D1029495

Tunisia

From Carthage to Tomorrow

tunisia

Texts by Claude Roy

and Paul Sebag.

Photographs by Inge Morath,

André Martin and Marc Riboud.

The Orion Press, New York.

Translation by Deirdre Butler

Library of Congress Catalog Card Number N° : 62-10328
Printed in France.

Preface

I wish to offer to those I love the most precious gifts in which the sun may share. And if when I dive near the burning beach I am not lucky enough to bring up from the sea floor a marble Aphrodite whose profile and charming breasts have been worn by the salt and waves off the Mahedia coast, — tide, time and the Mediterranean aiding the Athenian sculptor whose work was so soon to be drowned for two thousand years with the trireme bearing his gifts to the Romans of Byzacium; and if I don't know the secret of the Gafsa children whom I've seen taking grass loops and catching the furtive lizards which puff out their soft white throats in the desert sun; and if I don't know the call of the Cap Bon hunters who can persuade falcons to perch on their wrists, the way an apt idea may perch on the hand of a happy man; if, before I pick it, autumn — just on the verge of winter — withers the jasmine flowers that perfumed the garden of Hammamet; if I have not been able to pluck the giant lemons, color of the blazing sun, from the gardens of the Ariana... then I shall give you the gift of a palm tree, and its fronds will be tributes to you.

Perhaps I'll choose the Djerba palm tree, the one that looked like a young man who'd walked to the very edge of the beach and had stopped surprised when the sea's whispering mingled with the rustling of his sheaf, so he strained his head forward, leaning, and the light breeze barely ruffling the waves said to him, "This blue, fresh thing murmuring and caressing itself as far as you can see, this we call the sea."

Or I may decide on the Toser palm, the tall date palm which rose straight from the rim of the spring with its roots deep in the same freshness which its branches spread over us — and Bechir who climbed up, his feet as wide as hands curving over the trunk scales to the cut where the pale milk was distilled, lagmi *which must be drunk near the scar in the tree flank just as spring water should be drunk at its source.*

Unless I let myself be deceived and then instead of a palm tree, I'll take a column in the ruins of Thuburbo Majus, a column crowned with the hint of a palm carved in stone, a column which never stopped pushing upward nor being surprised, even after twenty centuries of pushing, at having nothing to uphold but sky and fresh air, there where a lark hangs his song overhead at the precise vertical and where, long ago, the temple displayed its pediment.

But no, I shall bring none of these palm trees to you, they must be left to quiver in the wild island palm groves or in the oasis where from dawn to dusk the water keeper metes out the flow to the irrigation canals in the gardens, as serious a distributor of justice and as silent. The palm tree I'll give you is the one at Sidi Bou Said growing in the patio of that house whiter than white, on the edge of a sea bluer than blue. Its foliage spreads out above the terraced roof with the underside of the fronds sheltering man and the upper side reflecting the sun's stubborn course. That palm is so beautiful that it is hard to decide if the house were built to shelter it or if it were planted to shelter the house. It's part of the family, the quietest and most thoughtful servant; the children have caressed its trunk, pulled out tufts of its fur, torn its scales as they torture a faithful pet who simply turns his muzzle away when he's teased by them and pretends not to resent the insult, nor to suffer. This palm tree is yours, yours, the house in its shade, and the sea around belongs wholly to you. From palm branch to palm tree, from house to village, from village to Tunis, from the Sahel to the oasis, — in the end I would offer all Tunisia to you as a present instead of the one palm tree I'd thought I had chosen. It is a tiny country, but we were happy there and happiness has less need of spacious land than of open spaces which need no measuring. (" A man, " says a Southern proverb, " can find no freedom in his heart if he is not free under heaven. ") In showing it to you I shall be like the Emir of Kairouan's ambassadors who arrived one day at the court of the Emperor of China. The latter wanted to know where they came from, ordered a globe, and looked for Tunisia without finding it. At last a fly which had lighted on the globe flew away uncovering the Ifrikiya it had hidden. In my turn I have traveled over all China and also over this little peninsula prolonging Africa to the northeast. We are never anywhere but there where we are, except in our thoughts which, like running water brimming over a basin, always overflow when we think we contain them. Does the ant care about the length of a frontier, does a traveler care if a country is huge or small? An ant gives thanks to the sun, and man to whatever makes his heart beat.

At the edge of grey olive groves and the blond desert I stopped to stay in a house whose silence is still singing slowly in me. I should like to praise that dwelling as one might praise a perfect poem. I lived there barefoot, sometimes treading the foot-caressing thick carpets, sometimes the mute cold of the tiles. Each step was a delight. There I learned, when the sun was at the zenith and the blinds shut, to name every shade of white just as a gardener names a rose, which we simply call a rose, by its exact name. White? White like what? The iridescent white tinged with the pale blue of cupolaed ceilings? Or the dazzling white of whitewashed walls? Or the mineral white of cool marble slabs? Or the tawny whiteness, like an animal's eye, of the raw wool rugs? Or the turgid white of orgeat syrup when ice water changes it into sky, — overcast, cloudy, thick with cumuli? We think we mean something when we say the word, white. *But when my host went to a Hafsid chest studded with fine copper nails he took out an old manuscript of still another white, — that of the white page with the inscription,* Praise be to God. *Yes, praise be to God, if he created the whiteness which the cicadas around us are praising summer in brightness, a brightness of white fire.*

And when the sun has burned out its force, I shall wake you to lead you to the garden; it will catch its breath again with the sweet promise of evening freshness. I shall name the trees to you just as one introduces old friends to the girl one has chosen. I shall say to you, here is the lemon tree, here are the cypresses, and the almond trees, here is the pomegranate — its fruit bursting with the coming of fall, here are the purple bougainvilleas, and the climbing, pale-scented geraniums. Here are the orange trees with a hammock set up under them —

a net to catch dreams, — and the book forgotten there which you can leaf through, — it is, of course, a volume of the Quatrains of Omar Khayyâm. And do not tell me, if a gem-like peacock passes on the path trailing his tail like an Elizabethan metaphor, do not tell me that this is too much, that the excess of splendor and exquisite things suddenly depresses you and that you suddenly notice you would like an error, a lapse in taste, — as one hopes for a pistol shot in an over-civilized salon. Say nothing yet. At dusk we will saddle the little grey horses and gallop over the steppes towards the desert. The bare expanses will intoxicate us with emptiness, absence and with the true rest which empty spaces offer our hearts.

But you whispered to me just what my own thoughts were murmuring to me. On this earth there are too many men for whom extreme simplicity could never be a spiritual luxury since it is the bitter dominant of their lives. He who has everything searches for the pleasure of being happy with little, but he who has nothing is desperate because it is nothing. The Orient was the inventor of wisdom, since for so long it was poverty's predilection: this, hunger's Orient, extends from Calabria to Chili, and although South America still belongs to it, China is beginning to escape. Years ago in the Sahel I used to meet Bedouins chased by hunger from the South who had loaded their scrawny camels with an empty couscous pot, an empty oil jar, a basket of rags and the earthenware kanoun, *— for their tea which is so black and strong that it turns their heads and makes them forget the weakness of starvation. And I remember the police who were leading away the salt thieves in chains, and at the time of the rebellion, the pallid light of the military courtroom where, every morning they condemned, to death or for life, the hunger for dignity and the thirst for freedom. I can still hear the man who was out of a job, from the wattled village of Saïda Manoubia, saying to my friend who is a friend of the poor, " My wife and children are hungry and my wife has dried up like a leaf. If I were still single I'd steal. Does that surprise you? But you know the saying, ' If Iblis (the Devil) gives you something to eat, he'll be your brother.' " No, I haven't forgotten that, not the eyes of children with trachoma, their swollen stomachs, and their rickets, nor the little corpses wrapped in rags on litters on the way to the cemeteries. But now this is how things stand: poverty is at present a problem for the poor and the poor are a problem for each one of us. Freedom is first of all the freedom not to be irresponsible for the hunger of the famished, for the destitution of those who used to be naked. No, I shall never forget poverty, but already poverty is beginning to forget what it was...*

We shall live for a while, if you wish, in a village not far from the sea, and in the evening when the men come back from the olive groves and fishing boats, we will go for coffee at Boussadia's on the square. We will listen to the news of the day — the Mahjoubs' camel was stuck in a swamp near the dry oued and how hard it was to get him out; the shepherd, Hedi, has brought back from the fields a fricassee of curlews he caught in his traps; old Fredji discovered a swarm of bees in the fig tree in his garden; Bouchraï's camel is sick and the bonesetter, Djirad, cauterized his belly with a red-hot sickle. You will admire as I do the great courtesy of ordinary speech, — a blind man is called the seeing one; *a deaf man, the* one whose ear has a long entrance corridor; *a one-eyed man,* the complete one; *a coloured man,* he who is a little dark. *And when we say good-bye to old Bouzaouache, he will say,* " God be your safe-conduct. "

When we've had enough rest we'll take to the road again. It will offer you the desert, an old tanned lion hide; blue-black Bedouin tents; prickly pears along the dusty road to the beach; rain beating on palm trees like a metallic tattoo; an old Spanish fort on the shore of that sea which talks in all tongues; a holy man's tomb where women request that a boy be granted them; a village asleep during the dog days, the window blinds painted sky blue against the unbearably bright whitewashed walls; the grey of olive trees; the white circle on a red background of the flags flapping in the wind; the huge concrete dams of the Medjerda and the ancient stone cisterns whose water the Emir Abou Ibrahim joyfully drank before he died; the ochre and black sails of fishing boats in the gulf bordered by palm trees; Ghriba synagogue and its smell of incense; the Barbier mosque with its straw matting; in the souk the smell of the candles with the five-branched, silver papered holders to be lit for Jaïna and Bechir's wedding and the perfume of attar of roses; the slow, to and fro movement of the camels raising water from the well to the irrigation canals; the reddening kanouns, *in the evening, in the doorways; the sea cemetery at Sidi Bou Saïd with its humble gravestones, tiny and white, at the edge of the sea, at the edge of the sky, on the beaches of suspended time, the laughing, chatting children playing with knuckle-bones; the oasis and its oranges, apples, pomegranates, peaches, figs, red and white raspberries, cassia and sour limes — gardens which the gods of fresh water have offered to the sand.*

Then we will arrive at Kairouan, it will be morning. There is but one God, yet the Great Mosque has more than a hundred columns. The high places of stone and perfected proportions are never immobile decorations devised for a resting spectator. Great architecture is always scaled to, or measured by, man who sets himself to the rhythm of his own pace. The full beauty of Chartres cathedral, of Pekin's Temple of Heaven, of St. Mark's Square in Venice, of Prague's Hradschin, of Versailles or Vézelay can be entirely realized and revealed only when we walk. And so we will go forward, barefoot and quiet, on the straw mats laid on the floor, for I would like the fixity of the mosque to come to life in you. It will then be like the space around a mobile which a breath may bring alive. Before they begin to move, the one hundred and eighty columns are waiting for our slow progress through their forest. Then they will compose the perfect linking and connecting groups of a transcendent dance. Onyx, porphyry, sandstone and marble will invent a silent choreography for your eyes with infinite, happy combinations, a succession of studied, abstract mirages.

You will quickly see that the grace of this concert is both masterful and borrowed. Every column here was taken from a temple or some building of the past. Ancient times, — Rome,

Greece, and the Orient abandoned to the refined raids of the Aghlabid emirs the capitals and shafts of their ruins. Just as certain lines in Racine's tragedies or certain passages of Chateaubriand's prose are woven with borrowings and reminiscences, so the great Kairouan Mosque is woven with quotations and alterations, each become a part of the whole. Ziyadet Allah, Ibraham II, and their architects took material whereever they found it, in Roman or Byzantine ruins for the construction of their praise to God. Archeologists can inventory here the methods of architectural organization borrowed from Egypt, Iraq and the Hellenistic traditions of Africa or Syria. Moreover these elements which might seem unmatched have not simply produced a composite structure. The genius of the Aghlabid builders succeeded in integrating them and in making a synthesis out of discrepancies. Carthage, Hadrumetum, Utica, Corinthian capitals and lapis lazuli mosaics of Byzantium, Bagdad pottery, — all these various treasures have been blended and melted together. Great art can be the work of inspired thieves.

The day will finally come when we will have to leave. But I know that just before our departure you will ask me, " When will we come back?" The reasons one may have to see a country are pleasant, but what is important are the reasons which remain and make one want to return again, to stay. One may like a place; but it is with men one makes friends.

My friend, Bouzouache, the old man, often says that he is like an old pulley that has worn out innumerable ropes. This Arab saying reminds me of other folk images which hare always made me smile a little and dream a lot — you can't pull the wool over his eyes, you can't tell him any tales, you can't teach an old dog new tricks; he can't be had; and finally, of a wise man, " he's heard that song before." Although I know the expression probably means that the wise man knows it all so well that he doesn't listen to it and doesn't even hear it, I still like to interpret it a little differently. For I don't think wisdom is hard either of hearing or heart. Surely wisdom hears, above all, songs made by men, by life, by happiness and the sadness of understanding, by love. To know the song means knowing everything too well, except the song itself, and music.

I don't know if I've heard them all too often, all the songs. I am just beginning to know Tunisia a little. But I think I understand her songs: the roar of Halfaouine on the night of Ramadan when the barkers, the darboukas, *the reedy flutes and wild violins make all their noise; the breathing of the sea at Kerkenna; the wind when it rises in the oasis and rustles the palms like a swell whispered in the sky, the crunching of sand in the extreme South when you walk barefoot and it burns the soles of your feet, the call of the muezzin when the sun is setting over Sidi Bou Saïd, when the grey-blue flat sea is traversed by veins of wind, veins like the veins of marble or like an old velvet stuff where you drew with your finger here and there against the grain. I have heard all sorts of music in Tunisia, the calls of the street vendors in Tunis in at dawn, the rag man crying on four notes, " Ro...ba...vec chia!" the tinker and the fresh mint man, the kerosene seller's horn, the foghorns of ships entering the harbor, the dry canter beating the ground of the thoroughbreds of the Sahel riders, the camels' bleating at the city walls, the popular singers whining through the bazar radios, the longed for tap-tap of rain on the nomad's tents, and later, the hurricane of half a million people, from La Goulette to Dar El Bey, shouting,* "Bourguiba yahya!" *I can still hear Susa schoolboys droning out an Alphonse Daudet text and Zitouna students enlarging their comments on the Koran, my friend of El Djem reciting to me at night, in the patio paved with Roman mosaics, the Georgic verses on the Libyan shepherd,* (Quid tibi pastores Libyae, quid pascua versu prosequar...) *the student telling me in a low voice, in 1952, "My father has been deported to the South," the chant of the Bedouin girl begging in the market at Sfax, the Saturday prayer in Ghriba synagogue, the second-hand dealers of Bab Sidi Abdallah offering me a 1903 sewing machine or a bride's orangeflower tiara (how did it ever turn up here?), the swear words of Sicilians playing tarots in the cafés of Dry-Cleaner Street, the whistles of the boys of Al Djezira at the movies when the bad man of a western seems to be gaining on the herd with his thundering pistols, the aged, literate Arab in his villa at Hammamet reading aloud to me the moral sentences of Imân Suhnoûn, or the Maltese porter insulting the Arab taxi driver, or the camel boy's call, " Zâa-Zâa!" which brings the tottering beasts to their feet at the stopping place. Yes, I think I know what fruits and songs, what murmurs and noises rise from Tunisian ground. And if I am asked why I like to live there, I can list several pleasures, but finally, there is one which sums up all the others: the pleasure of living among people who've heard the song before, who know what it's all about — and especially what the rope-fretting pulley is about.*

There is no man here who has not inherited the common experience of a people who have heard, seen and done everything and yet have kept — after shuttling through the rainbow — a taste for shades of meaning, a people who have heard it all, time and again, and yet have preserved an ear for music; they have rolled like stones that gather no moss but have been able to acquire on the way a lovely lustrous gleaming polish like the pulley-who-has-heard-the song-of-ropes-and-waters.

One always risks ridicule if one tries to explain the subtlety of a Tunis urchin's smile by the ancestors he knows nothing of, or the intricate genealogy which makes a Marsa bus driver heir to Aterians, Capsians, Libyans, Berbers or Numidians, Phoenicians, Romans, Vandals, Byzantines, Arabs, Aghlabids, Fatimids, Zeirids, Hilalians, Almohads, Hafsids, Normans, Spaniards, Turks, Frenchmen, Sicilians, and Maltese who in forty centuries have made Tunisia. No, to be precise, it is the Arabs who, over the centuries have left the deepest imprint on the ground of Ifrikiya. However, all the other influences, meetings, and comings and goings have enriched the Arab heritage, have fed it, had compromised with, and are compromised by, it.

There are nations whose fanaticism has vanished or has faded away due to the gradual extinction of its nourishment. With them intolerance is hardly a virtue since their faith is no longer a force of inspiration. Thus, nineteenth century China was inhabited by 400,000,000 Ernest Renan: effortless skeptics, unbelievers who asked no questions. The Chinese gods had been tired and exhausted for so long that they had not demanded anything, but in Tunisia, Allah, Jehovah, God the Father, and Our Lady of Trapani succeeded in vain to Tanit, Baal Hammon, Saturn, Demeter, the Aryan God, or to the Christ of the Byzantines. Their followers were never broadminded towards other faiths out of simple infidelity, but due to the necessary tolerance which cohabitation exacts. In spite of my awareness of the fact that racial intolerance, so violently opposed today, had existed in Tunisian daily life and that a Mohammedan could and did despise a Jew, a Christian believer the Mohammedan, that Tunisia was formerly no sentimental folk scene of universal harmony or of the peaceful co-existence of cults and beliefs, I still cannot prevent myself from thinking that this country today offers us a happy example, it shows us what tolerance is essentially — the fruit hard to come by, rare and beautiful, of the force of circumstances. *Yesterday Tunis seemed to me like the ship taken by the fifteenth century Dutch traveler, Adorne, " On this vessel there were a hundred Moors, men and women; some were merchants who had taken on a cargo of olive oil others were pilgrims who were to disembark at Mecca. There were also some Jews on the boat and the upshot was that there were three holidays a week on board, Christians on Sunday, Jews on Saturday, and Moors on Friday. " Tunis today, — but that's another story.*

I shall ask Mohammed to tell it to you. Perhaps he can. It is hard, however, to explain history when it is your own story; to tell it when telling it means explaining what one is. Mohammed has a thin silhouette and an agile mind. He is subtle, proud, sometimes touchy and always excitable. He knows how to smile; he knows how to listen and especially how to listen in order to learn. He was among the young men described in the Residence bulletins with the vague term, " anti-French elements ". However, he speaks better French than anyone, and with delight; he knows by heart as many poems by Baudelaire and Valéry as by Ibn Rachîq and Abou-l-Qâsim Chabbi. He does not want his children to forget France, nor his nation to break with the West and he is pleased that French is still one of the two languages officially taught in the State schools of the Tunisian Republic. He speaks a literary Arabic, the Arabic of the fellahs of Djerba, his island birthplace, as well as the Arabic of Tunis back streets. And he speaks varieties of French — university French, the French of jails (where he has spent some time) and the French of technicians whose disciplines and secrets he is studying passionately so as to build in Tunisia workers' housing projects, schools, and factories. For Mohammed is an architect, as you will speedily discover. He dreams of a Tunisia under whose sun will rise thousands of new dwellings and entire new sections of cities. He thinks so intensely of all this that occasionally I scold him — not because he is deserting our culture, but because he so violently wishes to assimilate it — even if it means the ruin of his own. I always want to stay his hand when he peremptorily draws exaggeratedly wide avenues which might destroy a very noble past. He loves his country with a downright kind of love whereby bulldozers proudly threaten ancient mosques. But you will do what I have done — forgive him for his occasionally iconoclastic daring and enthusiasm. He will take you one day to the sections of Tunis where only yesterday wattled huts were stagnating in filth and poverty, with the polluted water of old wells, the smoke of miserable fires, little girls weighed down with the jerry cans of water duty. He will show you the things which are so dull in "social" documentaries, a modern housing project, with its apartments by the hundred, running water on all floors, with clean children coming back from school. Mohammed will say to you, "I built that," and he will smile. And to whom I love I shall have given the most precious of gifts, a living person, a friend, a man on earth there where hope is still alive.

Claude Roy.

If, around truth,
A nation closes its ranks,
It then may hasten
Or slacken the progress of time.
Abou-l-Qâsim Chabbi.

Map of North Africa. XVIIth century. ►

Description of Barbary

In that part of the world which Geographers call Africa lies Barbary, extending on the West beyond the straits of Gibraltar from the Atlantic Ocean with the Canary Islands and Mount Atlas, to the East near Egypt all along the coast of the Mediterranean Sea. South across the deserts Barbary extends to the country of the Negroes, formerly called Interior Numidia, now Bildulgerid, in the great Atlas mountains. On that side Barbary includes the regions of Numidia where Carthage once existed, where now one finds the city of Tunis, the two Mauritanias together — made famous by the kingdoms of Tremessan, Bougie, Constantine and Bone and which today are those of Algiers, Coucque, Fez and Morocco.

To the East is Tripoli including almost all the country of Barca as far as Egypt, and save for outer Libya, Cyrenaica and Marmarica are also within its frontiers. Barbary is not equally temperate throughout and thus not equally fertile, since its diameter is approximately eight hundred leagues long whether one goes East, West, South or North, its produce is also unequally recommendable, and also the temperament of its climate. The purest air is found along the Mediterranean coast, from the Straits to Egypt, the best in all Barbary. However, in regard to the other regions lying inland and to the South, there is no doubt of their intemperate climate and excessive heat; they are utterly sterile and unfruitful. Therefore no one can inhabit their sand expanses and vast stretches of country and it can be accurately stated that they are true deserts for reasonable creatures, though not for quadrupeds or reptiles; nowhere in the world can one see more lions, leopards and tigers, nor more snakes and dragons of every variety. It is true that in compensation for this litter of savage and venomous beasts the country has the advantage of possessing an abundance of excellent horses whose tremendous speed and marvelous facility in handling place them in high esteem everywhere.

R.P. Pierre Dan.

MER
ME
ISLE DE MAIORQVE
SOLLARI
LAGALITA
PANTELARIA
LINUSA
MALTA
LAMPIDOSA
TVNIS
TRIPOLI
GOL
NVBIA DISERTA
AFRI
CA
A R B A

Aerial view of the village of Nefta, north of Chott El Djerid.

The perils of Chott El Djerid

One of the marvelous deeds of Ifrikiya was told to me by the cadi Abou Ruh' Isâ ez Zawâwi and by 'Abd Allah es Salalhi. Between Toser, capital of Djerid, and Bichri of the country of Nefzâwa, there are enormous marshes extending southward to the Sahara's unknown paths. In the middle of these salt marshes towards the north a road is open to travelers and allows those who are pressed to cross them for a short distance without risking their lives; it is a narrow road that Allah made to permit a dry crossing in the midst of the sebkha. If a voyager leaves the path, be it only by a hand's breadth, he falls into the swamp, deeper and deeper, disappears leaving no trace and no possibility of ever knowing anything. His companion may watch him sink without being able to help and without daring to hold out his hand for fear of sinking in with him. It is a fearful place for death, a salt marsh without water ! How many horses, camels and men who have left the road have perished ! On either side of the road wooden pickets are planted, the road runs between them, and if they were not there, travelers would perish unaware, " Half-way on the road crossing the sebkha, " said ez Zawâwi, " there is a free open space where travelers may sit down and rest. I followed that path and have seen it with my own eyes. " " We came, " said es Salalhi, " to the edge of the marshes but did not penetrate them for we were afraid. "

Al- 'Omarî.

Acqueduct from Zaghouan to Carthage.
Construction begun under Emperor Hadrian.
(IInd century A.D.)

The Acqueduct and the Berber Princess

When the Romans undertook the conquest of the country it was governed by a wise Berber monarch. But its armies could not resist the shock of the invaders and our monarch finally had to yield. However this ruler had a daughter who was said to be astonishingly beautiful. As soon as the Roman leader saw her he fell deeply in love and asked for her hand. The Berber princess who had a proud and noble soul refused to become the wife of the man who had enslaved her country. " Ask me for whatever you wish and I shall deposit it at your feet, but consent to share my life, " said the Roman leader. And the princess replied, " Let the united waters of the Zaghouan and the Djouggar be brought to Carthage without touching the earth, and I shall then consent. " She believed, poor child, that her consent would depend on an impossible condition. But for the Romans nothing was impossible and their leader ordered the construction of the most remarkable acqueduct anyone had ever seen.

One by one the arches, of which the ruins are still visible, rose towards the sky. At last the day came when, through the conduits they supported, flowed the waters of the Zaghouan and the Djouggar conjugated by the forces of men. The Roman leader then led the princess to this wonder of the world built for her. In order to admire fully the Roman masterpiece the princess asked if she could climb to the top of one of the arches. As soon as she reached that height she looked over the country of her birth, flung herself into space and was killed.

A Tunisian legend.

Pages 22/23 : *Wahabite mosque and holy man's chapel, Djerba Island.* ▸

Naive representation on Bedouin pottery.

Khamsa : *Amulet against the evil eye.*

Tunisian riddles

She is a very patient girl
Whose keys are male;
Without her, ramparts would not be built
And no ships would put to sea.

The hand

Street in Toser.

It is and is not,
It can cross water without getting wet,
Strike it with a sword, and it will not crack. — Shade

A coffer of saffron pouring out over the land
Of which no one can be master, neither bey nor sultan. — The Sun

Moslem cemetery at Monastir.
In the background, the Ribât, a fortress built at the end of the VIIIth century.
to assure the defence of Ifrikiya.

In the name of the Lord
Clement and Merciful

This is the tomb of 'Abd Allah, son of Muhammad, son of Yahiâ, son of 'Abd al-Rahmân, son of Qaîs, al-Ru'ainî. He died on Monday, 20 jumâdâ I of the year 306. He was born in the year 215.*

He died a witness to the fact that there is no other divinity than God in his unity, that Muhammad is his Servant and his Envoy, that Paradise is a reality, the fires of Hell realities, that the hour of Judgment will come without a doubt and that the Lord will resuscitate those who are in their tombs.

They covered my tomb near the road and said farewell to me. For him who is buried, there are no more friends.

Funeral inscription. Xth century.

* The departed lived from 830 to 918 in the Christian era.

Dates, wealth of the South. ▸

Pomegranates

Nathanaël, shall I speak to you of pomegranates?
They were sold for a few pennies at the Oriental fair,
On reed trays where they had fallen,
And you could see some rolling in the dust
Which naked children gathered.
The juice is tart like the juice of unripe raspberries.
The flowers are waxen,
The same color as the fruit.

Sections of hives, guarded treasure,
Richness of savor,
Pentagonal architecture,
The shell splits, the seeds fall,
Seeds of blood in azure bowls,
And some like drops of gold on plates of enameled bronze.

André Gide.

Roman mosaic, Susa Museum.

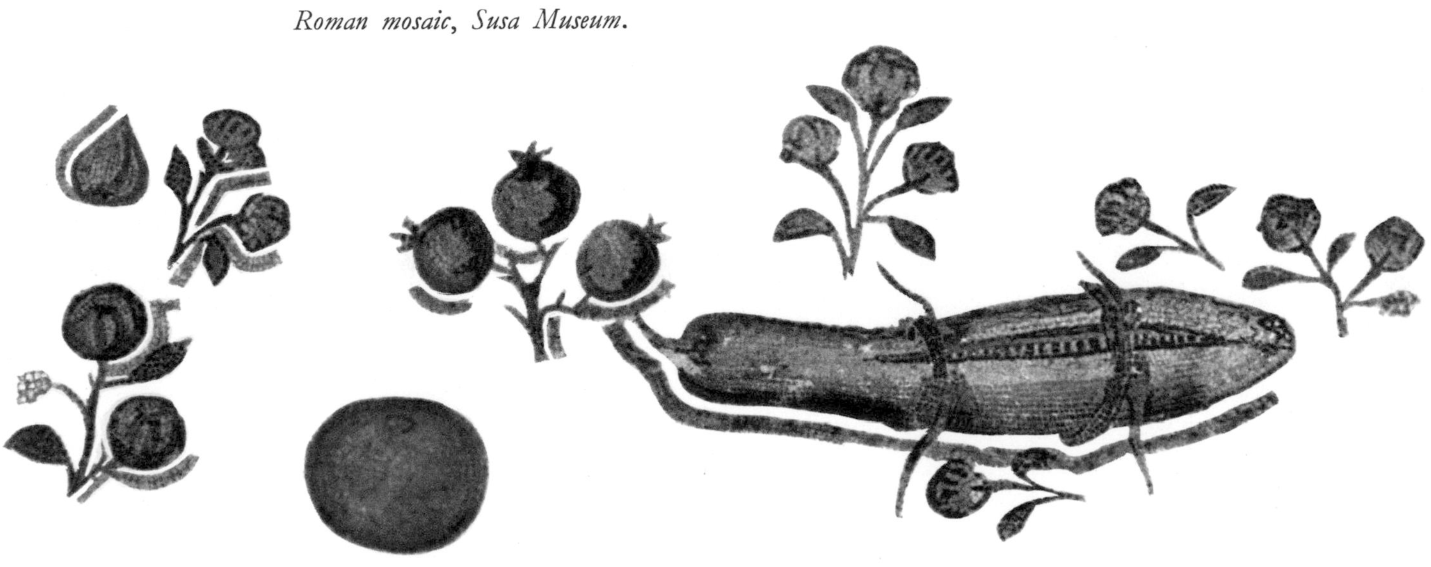

Squash, apple, figs, pomegranates and rosebuds.

Yamoun the potter

Decorative motif in plaster relief.

When the laborious dance is over and the flexible roll free of its stones is placed on the wheel, Yamoun jumps lightly to his place. He murmurs the humble prayer which sanctifies any task, " In the name of God ! " and the mystery begins.

The wheel, the maoun, is the very same that was used more than four thousand years ago by the earliest Egyptian artisans.

It is the beginning of a world. The shade is pierced by a single dazzling ray which sometimes makes the flies shiver.

Pushing with his foot, Yamoun gives his wheel its circular movement, the movement of the stars, the principle of all birth. Then he takes the lump of clay with both hands, as if he were clasping a face to kiss it. And what suddenly happens ? A flower of earth rises, rises and opens. The man hardly seems to touch it. He follows it as it climbs, he pats it, he contains it with astonishment. Like a god, Yamoun is observing his own creation. From time to time he dips his fingers in a little trough full of liquid mud and caresses his creature.

This force of gyration, this movement seems to divine all the wishes and thoughts of the artisan, it expresses them rapidly - revealingly. If Yamoun is inattentive for a mere second, the clay escapes and shows his distraction. If he tries to make it too perfect, the object grimaces and revolts. But Yamoun is an intelligent god, he is creating according to ancient laws.

The work suddenly appears finished. The magic wheel is prompter than desire. With a single pull of thread the vase is detached from the base. An offering. Careful hands pick it up. Is it real ? It has risen so quickly from the original earth that, to make it, one might believe it would suffice to dream of it.

Georges Duhamel.

◀ *Guellala potter, Djerba Island.*

Pages 32/33 : *Amphorae and potter's oven at Guellala.* ▶

Decorative motif, plaster relief.

Oh, Wall, spin me a thread

O wall, spin me a thread,
The wall says, what is my power,
What are my powers?
Since the rat runs through me.

O rat, spin me a thread,
The rat says, what is my power,
What are my powers?
Since the cat eats me up.

O cat, spin me a thread,
The cat says, what is my power,
What are my powers?
Since the dog frightens me.

O dog, spin me a thread,
The dog says, what is my power,
What are my powers?
Since my picket holds me prisoner.

O picket, spin me a thread,
The picket says, what is my power,
What are my powers?
Since the fire devours me.

O fire, spin me a thread.
The fire says, what is my power,
What are my powers?
Since water extinguishes me.

A weaver spools his thread.

O water, spin me a thread,
The water says, what is my power,
What are my powers?
Since the bull drinks me.

O bull, spin me a thread,
The bull says, what is my power,
What are my powers?
Since the knife cuts my throat.

O knife, spin me a thread,
The knife says, what is my power,
What are my powers?
Since the blacksmith whets me fine.

O blacksmith, spin me a thread,
The smith says, what is my power,
What are my powers?
Since death carries me away.

A game sung
by the women weavers of Djerba.

A Carthaginian speaks *

Ythalonimualonuthsichorathisimacomsyth
Chymlachchunythmysthalmyctibaruimischi
Liphocanethythbythiiadoedinbynuthii
Byrnarobsyllohomaloniuybymisyrthoho
Bythlymmothymnoctothlechantidamachon
Yssidobrimtyfel yth chylys chon, chem, liphul,
YthbynimysdiburthinnochotnuAgorastocles
Ythemanetihychyrsaelycochsitnaso
Byuniidchilluchiligubylimlasibiththim
Bodyalytheraynnynnuyslymmoncothiusim
Exanolimvolanussccuratimistiacumesse
Concubitumabellocutinibeathelacantinoca
Enuseshuiecsilihcpanessearthidamasconalemindubertefelonobuthume
CeltumcomucrolufulatenimavosouberhenthyachAristoclem
Etteseanachnasoctelialelicosalemusdubertermicompsuestipti
Aodeaneclictorbodesiussumlimnimcolus.

Plautus.

* *This is not merely an incoherent and burlesque parody but is a true Punic tongue, written in the Latin alphabet — with the vowels simply as they are pronounced.*

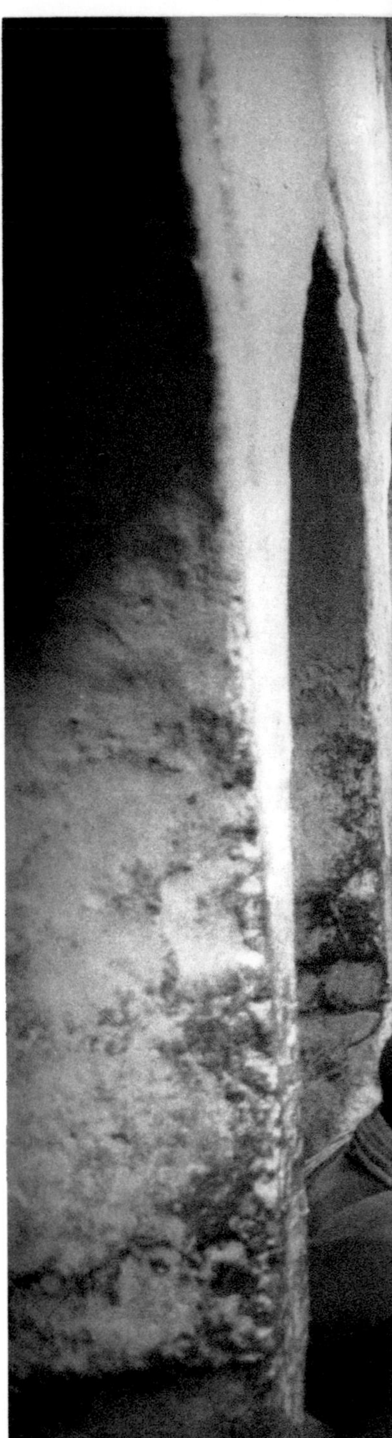

Djerba souks.

◀ *Carthaginian clay mask.*
Placed in a tomb it protected
the dead against evil spirits.

Decorative motif on a door at Hammamet.

Wisdom

Work, you will bite your bread;
Continue doing nothing, you will regret.

If you are gifted for cutting clothes,
Learn how to use scissors;
If you are gifted for sewing,
Learn how to use needles.

Ancestral fortunes disappear,
A manual trade lasts.

A trade is a bracelet of gold.

◂ *A woman weaver of Kairouan rugs with her loom.*

Tunisian proverbs.

Tunisian jewels. Chains, necklaces, earrings. ▸

I see my girl, my friend

I see my girl, swaying softly like a cypress.
Her hair, black like Drid feathers covered with jewels.
I see her tattoo marks freshly blue, her forehead gleams like a sun.
Her cheeks are roses under her heavy earrings.
Her nose is like the beak of the terkelia bird.
Her neck is like a gazelle's, the silver necklaces on her shoulders are less radiant than her smile.
There I see her breasts, each independent, pointing forward.
Happy necklaces caressing them, happy jewels adorning them!
Her thighs are like the columns of temples before Islam.
Her legs shine like crystal, her feet are like a wild pigeon's.
I hear her anklets ringing against each other.
I should like to be the pin in your hair, your earring, the necklace on your breasts, the circlet at your feet.
Praise be to the Lord, the Generous, the Most High, he has created my friend, my girl who shines more brightly than the jewels I have offered her as gifts.

Folksong, Southern Tunisia.

A villa near Hammamet.

And on earth you see pieces, different
in their nature though next each other,
gardens with vineyards, wheatfields,
palm trees, alone or clustered together.

They are watered by the same water,
it is we who make some superior
to others, in regard to meaning and taste.
Assuredly, in this there are signs
for men gifted with sight.

Koran XIII, 4.

Details of a Roman mosaic.
Lemon, ducks, fruit basket,
pomegranates and flowers.
Susa Museum.

Pottery tiles. Andalusian tradition.
Dar Hussein, Tunis.

Tunisian courtesy

May your day be blessed.
May your day be fortunate.

May your day be good.
May your day be like milk.

Be in good company.
The Lord be with you.

God keep you.
May God protect you.

May the Lord grant you a happy evening.
May the Lord grant you peace and a happy evening.

May your evening be pleasant.
May God give you a pleasant evening.

Greetings to you.
To you greetings, along with divine pity and blessings.

Your visit is a blessing on us.
God bless you.

May your night be happy.
May your night be blessed.

May you find happiness in the morning.
May you find happiness and peace in the morning.

We are leaving you in the Lord's care.
May the Lord be your safe conduct.

Rest in God's protection.
Rest in peace.

Pages 46/47: *Monastir, from the top of Ribât tower.*

The founding of Kairouan

On his expedition against Ifrikiya, 'Uqba b. Nâfi' came to the valley of Qaîrawân. There he spent the night with his companions. In the morning when he stopped at the valley entrance he cried, "Dwellers of the valley, leave, for we are stopping here!" Three times he shouted this order. Immediately, snakes, scorpions and multitudes of other unknown animal species left. The warriors stood watching this flight from early morning until the heat became too oppressive, and then when they saw that all had vanished they settled in the valley. Forty years after this event the inhabitants of Ifrikiya could never have found either a snake or a scorpion even if they had been offered a thousand dinars!

Ibn 'Abd Al-Hakam.

◂ *The Great Mosque of Kairouan. Courtyard and the front of the prayer hall. IXth century.*

Tunisian riddle.

A lion which eats men
And leaves nothing of him whom he devours.
He eats glorious robes as if they were rags
And leaves not a single fiber of flesh.

The tomb

The great mosque of Kairouan. Minaret, seen from the cemetery of the Awlâd Farhân. ▸

The Great Kairouan Mosque. The mihrâb. ►
Marble, with a painted wood vault,
tiles and, within, openwork decoration.
IXth century.

Pages 52/53:
Stuffs spread out, women in sefsari,
a difficult choice.

A virtuous cadi

When Abou Koraib was judge, or cadi, at al-Qaîrawân, he lived in the village known as d'as-Sinjârî. When he wanted to go to the cathedral mosque he drove his donkey before him and when he left the mosque he rode his donkey home. He could sometimes be seen walking to the mosque in mud which was nearly knee deep. " Why don't you ride? " people asked, " No," he answered, "this is the way a man who is approaching God should walk : he walks with a humble attitude and with humility. " And sometimes people saw him all alone in the mosque and said, " Why don't you leave? " "But then who would replace me if someone desperate with worry were to look for me and not find me? " Ahmed ben Bohlul said that Abou Koraib sometimes found the solution to a problem in the middle of the night. He would then go in the dead of night to the house of the man whose rights he had recognized and knock at the door. He would make him come out and order him to assemble those neighbors who were men of honor as witnesses. " Why don't you let it go until tomorrow morning? " the man would say. " But if I die tonight, " replied Abou Koraib, " Wouldn't I be responsible for your loss of your rights? "

Abou-l-'Arab.

Market day in the great square of Houmt Souk.
Susa market seen from the Ribât.

Honor

Everything is sold at the market
At its price, without discussion,
Except your honor as a man among men.
Torn honor cannot be mended
Even with real silk:
The cloth gave way, you can put your fingers
through it.
Honor among the well born
Is a brilliant, clear crystal.
If it breaks
There is no mender who can mend it.

Tunisian folk poem.

◂ *Dress and ornaments of Mahedia.*

Weave, weave me a rug

Weave, weave me a rug of softest wool
So that on it the gazelle may stand, the dark eyed girl, whose glance, like a sharpened spear wounded my liver.

Weave, weave me a rug of softest wool
So that she who is light as a partridge may walk on it, she whose smile dries the saliva in my mouth.

Weave, weave me a rug of softest wool
So that the radiant Halima, like a rose opened in the center of a bouquet,
May lie down on it and sleep.

Weave, weave me a rug of softest wool
And I shall taste her like a first fresh fruit. I shall pluck off her petals.
I shall choose between two apples and unfasten her belt.

Southern Tunisian folksong.

Mecca in the center of the Islamic world.
Taken from a portulan by the
Tunisian cartographer Ibn Mohamed Ech Charfi of Sfax.
XVIth century.

A dramatic pilgrimage

In the year 1175* a number of respectable citizens of Béjà, Bedouins, Tunis notables, merchants and rich people met to make a pilgrimage to Mecca together and for that purpose rented a ship belonging to Christians at Doublet-Benadi which had never put to sea. Among the passengers were three notables from Béjà, a son of the sheik Touati, as well as lawyers and business men of the same city. The boat left with a huge cargo of Tunisian merchandise and several passengers; it was the season of the equinox and after two or three days at sea, the ship was caught in a dreadfully violent storm which wrecked all the boats moored in the coastal harbors and kept the pilgrims' craft heeled way over for several days. They had utterly lost their bearings when suddenly one evening the captain saw land ahead. He began to weep and beat his breast and told his passengers to prepare for death. Lamentations and cries rang through the ship. The captain tried to steer and set a sail, but it was torn in two by the wind. Since they were coming in closer and closer to the shore, the captain first threw out one anchor, then another heavier one, and the boat was stopped; night was falling but the wind raged on furiously. When the ship's course was halted, the passengers were wonderfully relieved and congratulated themselves on their escape from death; some tried to sleep, others gathered on deck. Suddenly they heard the noise of a huge shock, like a thunderbolt; the goods in the hold tumbled into the sea and the water began to rise in the ship. All the terrified passengers rushed up on deck — some were killed instantly, others clung to the sheets. The prow was wrecked on a wave-beaten rock, everyone on deck was killed as well as those who were below or in the hold. Out of three or four hundred passengers only fifty or sixty survived, who remained until morning on the derelict crushed by the storm. At daybreak they saw that the shipwreck had taken place near a village of Sahel called Bekalta. In the memory of men nobody had ever seen a ship wrecked on the way to Mecca; those wrecks only occurred on the return course.

Seghir Ben Youssef.

* 1175 of the hegira corresponds to the year 1762 of the Christian era.

Votive stele to Saturn, discovered at Maktar. Bardo Museum.

The life of a peasant in Roman Africa

I was born of poor parents, my father had neither an income nor his own house. From the day of my birth I always cultivated my field; neither my land nor I ever had any rest. When the season of ripened harvests came I was the first to cut my thatch; and in the country when you would see the groups of harvesters who hire themselves out around Cirta, the Numidian capital, or in the plain dominated by the mountain of Jupiter, I was first to harvest my field. Then I left my country and for twelve years I harvested for another under a fiery sun; for eleven years I was head of a harvesting team and mowed the wheat in the Numidian fields. Thanks to my labors and since I was content with little, I finally became owner of a house and land: today I live at ease. I have even obtained honor, I was named to sit in the senate of my city: the modest peasant became censor. I have seen my children and grandchildren grow up; my life has been occupied, peaceful, and honored by all.

Maktar inscription.

Pagan gods

It is not said that the gods *created*, but rather that they *discovered* all things necessary to life, However, a thing one discovers is a thing that already existed and a thing that already existed should not be attributed to him who discovered it but to him who created it; since it existed before it was found. Thus if Liber* is a god because he introduced the vine we are unfair to Lucullus, who was the first to bring cherries from Pontus for the Romans and to make them known in Italy, not to have deified him as the author of a new fruit, to have made it known...

Tertullian.

*Ancient Italic divinity identified at Dionysos.

Hermès of Dionysos.
Mahedia undersea finds.
Bardo Museum.

Plowing season

Plowing with a swing plow, Cap Bon.

After Adam had been driven out of paradise for his sins, he finally felt strong pangs of hunger. He spoke of it to the Archangel Gabriel, " Between my skin and my bones, " he said, " I feel a certain tingling! " The angel understood, " It's hunger, and I am going to find you a remedy." In reply to his prayer two russet oxen came down from heaven along with tools for ironmongering and plow construction. And so it is that now when the Bedouins go to the landowners in the Kairouan region to inquire if it's time to plow, they ask the following question, " Have the two come down? " in allusion to the story of the two oxen who came down from heaven.

A. Renon.

The Bowl of Nefta.
Out of a huge funnel in the midst of the sands,
rise springs giving life
to this corner of the desert.

Forces of green and growing nature

The oases of Gabes, Toser and Nefta are all of much the same size, each consisting of some six or seven thousand acres of cultivated ground, and are all three remarkable for their numerous and copious springs. In the middle of the desert, suddenly, a hundred fountains come welling out of the sand; rivers run, a network of little canals is dug. An innumerable forest of date palms springs up - a forest whose undergrowth is corn and roses, wines and apricot trees, olives and pomegranates, pepper trees, castor-oil trees, banana trees, every precious plant of the temperate and the sub-tropical zones - No rain falls on these little Edens - except on the days of my arrival - but the springs, fed from who knows what distant source, flow inexhaustibly and have flowed at least since Roman times. Islanded among the sands, their green luxuriance is a standing miracle. That it should have been in a desert, with here and there such islands of palm trees, that Judaism and Mohammedanism took their rise is a thing which, since I have seen an oasis, astonishes me. The religion which, in such a country, would naturally suggest itself to me would be no abstract monotheism, but the adoration of life, of the forces of green and growing nature. In an oasis, it seems to me, the worship of Pan and of the Great Mother should be celebrated with an almost desperate earnestness—The nymphs of water and of trees ought surely, here, to receive a passionate gratitude. In the desert, I should infallibly have invented the Greek mythology. The Jews and the Arabs discovered Jahweh and Allah. I find it strange.

Aldous Huxley.

Gorgon's head. Roman mosaic. Susa Museum.

Date picking in the Degache oasis.

An oasis

Fons abundat, largus quidem, sed certis horarum spatiis dispensatur inter incolas. Palmae ibi praegrandi subditur olea, huic ficus, fico punica, illi vitis: sub vite seritur frumentum, mox legumen, deinde olus; omnia eodem anno; omniaque aliena umbra aluntur.

There a spring gushes forth, generously, it is true; but its water is distributed to the inhabitants one by one at fixed times. There under a tall palm tree the olive tree hides, under the olive tree the fig tree, under the fig tree the pomegranate, and under the pomegranate, the vine; under the vine, wheat is sown, then vegetables and at last pot-herbs, all in the same year; and all these varieties grow each in the shade of the other.

Pliny the Elder.

Gabes oasis.

What do donkeys dream of?

Exhausted by the long road, straining under the load, harassed by blows, limping and hobbling with my bruised feet, I finally reached the edge of a little winding stream with soft water; that was a piece of luck to snatch at and I thought of letting myself fall forward with all my weight, skilfully folding my legs, firmly determined, even if I were beaten, not to get up and go on again.

Apuleius.

Christian bas-relief. ▸
The Good Shepherd.
Susa Museum.

The mouse and his bride

A small mouse took a young mouse in marriage. He was eager to satisfy her every whim, "Where shall I put you, oh, tray of roses!" and to ask for more wishes to fulfill, and to offer her delicacies and ornaments. They lived ever so happily, wonderful days that do not count in life.

One day his young bride said, " Oh, master of my house... I have wonderful news for you if you'll give me a present... " "Anything," " Well ," said she, " I'm expecting a child. " Her husband leaped with joy, swallowed the wrong way and choked, " Anything you desire, just say, I'm ready. " " I should like to go to the baths and on my return I'd like to find a good plate of *hassou** bubbling and swimming in sauce and deliciously spicy. "

" For you I'd bring the moon... Run along, fetch your haïk and your veil, I'll take you to the hammâm. "

The bride got up, put on her haïk and her veil and set off with her husband. He led and she followed and trotted along to the pond.

" Into the water you go, my sweet, " he said, "have a lovely bath and while you're washing I'll bring the leaven so we can make the *hassou.*" Mrs. Mouse climbed down into the pond to take her bath and Mr. Mouse went off to the houses to look for leaven.

The little bride swam around gaily. But when finally she wanted to climb out of the pond, the bank was too steep and high. She climbed and fell down again and again until she was exhausted. She shouted and called and wept and was terrified of drowning.

A rooster strutting like a threatening lion happened to come by. Little Mrs Mouse called, " Ho there, noble cavalier without a mount and with only your spurs as harness, - you who carry a stick in your mouth, pull me out of this pond and my husband will give you a generous reward. "

The rooster came near and held out his beak, but the little lady mouse protested, " A strange man's lips touching me - it would sinful! " He opened his wing, "But how would I ever hold on to feathers ? " He held out his foot. " Never, your nails would scratch me. " So the rooster went away abandoning the little mouse.

Then a toad came by, " Ho, there my Lord Toad, " she cried, " Get me out of this pond and I'll give you a dumpling. " The toad approached, " Raise your head higher and I'll get you out. "

" Oh, no, " said Mrs. Mouse, " I fear for my curls and then everyone will laugh at me. "

" And how do you expect me to help you out without touching you? That's something no man could possibly do. "

" Go quick, " she said, " and call my husband, Mr. Mouse! " " But how shall I recognize him in all the crowd of mice and rats ? " " Go find them and shout, *'Ho, Mr. Mouse, come here, leaven-looting pilferer, run to your pretty young wife, who in the pond is losing her life!' "*

The toad rushed to the crowd of mice and shouted. *'Ho, Mr. Mouse, come here, leaven-looting pilferer, run to your pretty young wife, who in the pond is losing her life! ' "*

From the depths of the *hassou* stewpot Mr. Mouse cried, " Oh, you who have just come from my darling wife, go tell her, 'your husband is in the pot; he plunged into it to take the leaven. Now he's caught and can't get out. He can't be saved. There's nothing to do!' ".

That is the fruit of greed. Learned men have somewhere written, " Overweening ambition may break your neck. "

Tunisian folk tale.

*Hassou *is a spiced porridge.*

El Hamma spring in Djerid.

Ceremonial haram *embroidered with gold and silver.* ▸

Pages 76/77: *In the cork oak forest of Khroumiria.*

The lion and the woman

Once upon a time near a deep dark jungle there was a village where a lion often came to steal sheep and attack people. One day the village elders decided to win the favors of the prince of beasts by sending him a woman messenger. They said to themselves, the king of animals will certainly respect the requests of a daughter of men. And this woman was named Sabra. So one day she went to the jungle to chop wood. The lion left his lair in search of prey. Sabra was terrified, frozen with fear, and more dead than alive, she begged him to spare her and also to spare her village. Unexpectedly, the royal personage, who was struck by the woman's words, began treating her with courtesy and affability. He even offered - all this took place at the time "when animals talked" - to help her chop wood. And every day Sabra went to the jungle, and every day the lion helped Sabra so that finally they were married and lived together for several years. The lion found game for their food, his wife prepared the dinner. And with her royal husband Sabra enjoyed a most delightful life.

One day the lion found her completely upset, "But what's happened to you today?" "It's been such a long time since I've seen my mother, let me go see her, I beg you." So the lion escorted the woman to the edge of the jungle, "I'll wait for you here. Come back in a few days." In the village her return set off a celebration, nobody talked about anything except Sabra and her lion. Some praised her brave husband, others found fault with him. And so the story goes and I could tell you more and more. "My husband is very good to me, he's as pleasant and nice as can be. I can only say good things about him. However, there is one thing I don't like: his breath is bad." The lion heard this - lions have very sensitive ears and can hear at a great distance. But Sabra didn't know that. After she spent some days with her mother, the woman returned to the jungle. At the edge the lion was waiting. They resumed their life and habits. And Sabra was taking her axe to go to work when the lion suddenly stopped her. "Strike me with your axe there, on my forehead between my eyes." — "Me, strike you, it's impossible! No, you've always been good to me, no, I can't." — "Strike me, I tell you or I'll be furious!" The lion roared. When a lion is in a rage it is dreadful. Sabra was so frightened by him that she struck him a blow with her axe just between his eyes.

The lion roared with pain. Jackals came to lick his wound. Sabra was horribly upset and snatched at the spider webs hanging in the crannies of the cave and made a bandage to stop, this blood. She found rags to make a real bandage, and every day the wound was better.

Finally one day it was cured. Sabra happily announced the total cure to her royal spouse, who replied: "The wound is cured, Sabra, and it no longer requires bandages: but, Sabra, cruel words remain at night and wake at morning." So saying, he leaped at her and devoured her.

Tunisian tale.

Votive steles at Baal Hammon-Saturn.
Open-air museum, Carthage.

Sacrifices at Baal Hammon-Saturn

Since they attributed to the gods the defeat they had just suffered*, the Carthaginians reproached themselves for having angered Saturn; formerly they had sacrificed children of the most important citizens to him but later they had abandoned this custom and secretly bought children for sacrifice to the god. Investigations revealed that many of the sacrificed children were substitutes. As they reflected on all this and watched the enemy camp just outside the walls of their city, they were overwhelmed with sudden superstitious terror and berated themselves for having neglected ancestral custom in regard to worship of the gods. They decided therefore to have a huge ceremony during which they would sacrifice two hundred children chosen from the most illustrious families, and some citizens under accusation volunteered their own children, at least three hundred of them. The sacrifice was carried out thus: there was a bronze statue of Saturn with his hands stretched out and down towards the ground so that the child placed in them rolled over and fell into a hollow pit with a fire inside. When Euripides described sacrificial acts in Tauride, he was probably referring to this ceremony, he had Orestes ask, " What tomb will receive me when I die? " " A sacred fire lighted in a great abyss in the earth. " It would seem that the ancient Greek myth according to which Saturn devoured his own children may be explained by this Carthaginian custom.

Diodorus of Sicily.

* At the end of the IVth century B.C. the Carthaginians were besieged by the Sicilian condottiere, Agathocle.

Menorah,
outlined in whitewash on a house at Hara Es Seghira.

Precepts of the Synagogue elders

Rabbi Meïr always said, do not devote too much time to business, but devote yourself also to study of the law and be humble with everyone. If you abandon study the of law in favor of worldly affairs the latter will not go well for you, but if you devote yourself to law study, your reward will be great.

Ben Bag-Bag said, turn the law over and over, examine it from every side, for it contains everything and alone the law will give you intelligence. Grow old in its study and never abandon it, you can do nothing better.

Pirke Aboth.

Rabbis of Hara Es Seghira.

Ghriba Synagogue at Hara Es Seghira.

The Remarkable One

A long time ago in these regions which were still deserts, there came a young woman of unequaled beauty and distinction. With her own hands she built a hut of branches and set out to live alone in it. Her modesty, reserve and her solitary life were sources of general wonder. And so she was soon called, " the Foreign woman ", " the Amazing One, " " the Extraordinary woman," *Ghriba,* in Arabic. It was true that her face reflected holiness and nobody tried to force her retreat or clear away the mystery of her existence.

One night the inhabitants of the neighboring village saw flames blazing above the hut, but as they were afraid that the Foreign Woman was practising magic and were paralyzed with terror, not one of them would go to her. And at last when finally a few decided to go and see, the hut was only a heap of ashes and in the midst of the last glowing reddened coals, they saw the young woman stretched out lifeless, but - oh, miracle, her face and body were intact and had been spared by the flames.

The villagers then understood that the Foreign Woman was a pure and holy woman. They blamed themselves severely for not taking charge of her, for not honoring her as they should have and, far worse, for not having gone to her aid in danger. After discussion they decided to build a synagogue on the site of the catastrophe with the hope of obtaining her forgiveness. And it is in her memory that the synagogue they built is called to this day Ghriba.

N. Slouchz.

Roman mosaic. Circus games: spectators. Bardo Museum.

Aerial view of El Djem. In the center, the amphitheater. IIIrd century. ▸

The Bloody Arena

As soon as Alypius had seen blood he drank deeply of its violence. Instead of looking away he watched the scene intently and unconsciously absorbed its rage; he was fascinated by these criminal combats and intoxicated by their bloody voluptuousness. He was not the same man who had come a little while ago, for he had become part of the crowd and a true companion of those who had brought him. What more is there to say? He watched, he yelled. He was wildly thrilled and went away in a sort of frenzy which drove him not only to return with those who had encouraged him but to lead them and bring along others.

St. Augustine.

Pages 86/87: *Roman ruins of Thuburbo Majus. Forum, Capitol and Temple of Mercury.*

*Tabella defixionis**

Roman theater at Dougga. IInd century. ▶

Stop them, chain them, weaken them; so that they cannot leave the stables, nor get through the hippodrome gate, nor make a single step forward on the track; and as for the men who are driving, tie up their hands, don't let them see, don't let them catch the reins or even stand up! Throw them out of the chariots, fling them to the ground, let the horses stamp on them! There's no time to waste, quick, quick!

Latin inscription

* The circus drivers took the *tabellae defixionum* to call for the gods' curses on their opponents.

Roman mosaic. Circus games: chariot in the arena. Bardo Museum.

In an ancient theater

What a big crowd I see gathered to hear me. I must congratulate Carthage for having so many friends of science, rather than excusing myself — a philosopher — for not refusing to make this speech. For these numbers correspond to the city's importance and the choice of the place to these enormous numbers. Moreover, at a meeting like this, we are not here to examine the marble pavements, the stage architecture, nor its decorative columns, the brilliant panelling, nor the half moon of the grandstand. And what difference does it make that in this place at other times a mime plays clown, an actor chats, a tragedian declaims or a tightrope dancer makes dangerous leaps, a barker roars and gesticulates or that all sorts of public players demonstrate their art to the crowd. Let us forget all that and now pay attention only to the audience's intelligence and the orator's tongue.

Apuleius.

The Sbeitla countryside; in the background the Capitoline temples of ancient Sufetula.

Libyan shepherds

Quid tibi pastores Libyae, quid pascua versu
Prosequar et raris habitata mapalia tectis?
Saepe diem noctemque et totum ex ordine mensem
Pascitur itque pecus longa in deserta sine ullis
Hospitiis: tantum campi jacet! Omnia secum
Armentarius Afer agit, tectum Laremque
Armaque Amyclaeumque canem Cressamque pharetram;
Non secus ac patriis acer Romanus in armis
Injusto sub fasce viam cum carpit, et hosti
Ante expectatum positis stat in agmine castris.

Shall I follow in my poem the Libyan shepherds
Stopping with them when they put up
Here and there a tent or hut?
Often both night and day, sometimes for a month,
The herd moves on, grazing,
Across interminable deserts without a single shelter,
So vast is the plain that flees underfoot!
House, gods, arms, Cretan quiver, Amyclean hound,
The African cowherd takes everything with him.
Thus the soldier on a campaign,
The admirable Roman soldier,
Carrying ancestral weapons on his back
Follows his route with this enormous load;
He presents himself to the enemy before the hour,
With his camp already pitched, he is ready for combat.

Virgil.

Pages 92/93: *Ulysses and the sirens: Roman mosaic. Bardo Museum.*

Paved street of the Roman Dougga. ▶

Carthage roads from the height of Sidi-Bou-Saïd.

The Trojans at Carthage

In this bay there is no need of moorings to fetter the vessels worn by the waves, no anchors hold them pinioned. This is where Aeneas once again mustered and urged landward the seven ships left him. And then it was that the Trojans, lured from their ships by their deep love of land, fell upon this coveted beach and on its very edge stretched out their bodies wasted by sea water.

Virgil.

The gardens of Graesse

After passing throught the cities of Syllecte and Hadramet we came to the city of Graesse*, about three hundred and fifty stades from Carthage. Here was the Palace of the Chief of the army of Vandals and the most beautiful Paradise of all those we knew, since it was watered by several fresh water streams and surrounded by a great forest making it incredibly lovely, as all abounded with innumerable fruit trees, then already green, and so leafy that our soldiers built their huts with these leaves and branches, and they ate so many fruits that they were intoxicated. Moreover, there was such profusion that they didn't spare them but were delighted with

◄ *Hammamet and its orchards.*

Venus, Roman mosaic.
Bardo Museum.

them all, satisfying all their senses since these fruits were so beautiful to see and so sweet-smelling that the soldiers always had their hands full.

Procopius.

* Presumably the gardens of Graesse, where the Vandal chief had his palace, were in the region of Hammamet.

Tunisian Riddle

A lightning streak in flight
Which bolts away from everyone.
It neither flies in the air,
Nor walks on the ground. A fish

Roman mosaic.
Fisherman with his rod.
Bardo Museum.

Palm tree on the Djerba shore.

The land of the Lotuseaters

The tenth day brought us to the shores of the land of the Lotuseaters — the people who live on only one food, a flower. On our arrival we landed, went to draw water, and quickly prepared our meal close by the hulls of the boats. Once we had satisfied hunger and thirst, I sent off three of my men to reconnoiter, — two especially selected by me, to whom I added a scout. They were only a little way off when they met the Lotuseaters who, far from planning murder, served them lotus. But just as soon as they tasted these honeyed fruits they lost all desire to return or bring news. I had to drag them, weeping, by force and place them one by one down under the benches in the bottom of the boats. Then I re-embarked the men who had remained faithful. No delay, all aboard, anchors aweigh! I was afraid that if they tasted those dates, the others would also forget the date of return.

Homer.

* Since ancient times the land of the Lotuseaters has been identified with the Island of Djerba.

Spanish expedition of 1560 against Djerba Island. Map by the Piedmontese cosmographer, Giacomo Gastaldi.

Djerba in the XVIth century

Djerba has neither castles, lands, nor towns, but only three or four hamlets; and other dwelling places are simply thatched huts scattered over nearly all the island. It is full of palm groves yielding countless dates, olive trees giving a fair amount of oil and many vineyards - more for harvests of raisins than for wine. There are also figs, pears, apples, plums, apricots, giant lemons, a kind of wild orange and some small gardens filled with fruit trees. Beyond that Djerba produces only barley, sorghum, lentils, beans, chick-peas and other vegetables. Livestock, large and small, comes from the continent. However there are many donkeys and camels on the island. There are also chameleons and rabbits. The inhabitants have very few horses. They weave with fine wool and make very beautiful *baracans* of a thin material, decorated with silk and longer than an ordinary rug.

A.F. Cirni.

Pages 102/103: *Djerba Island from the top of the Tourgueness lighthouse.* ▶

Basilica of St. Cyprian at Carthage.

The sorrow of Monique

But the reasons for my leaving Carthage for Rome You knew, Oh Lord, though You informed neither me nor my mother. My departure provoked the cruellest lamentations, for she wished to follow me all the way to the sea. She clung passionately to me, to sustain me or to leave with me. But I misled her by pretending I did not wish to leave a friend who was waiting in his turn for a favorable wind before

embarking. I lied to my mother, and to such a mother! And I fled. She refused to turn back without me. I had difficulty in persuading her to spend that night in the chapel of the Blessed Cyprian, very near our ship. And that very night I escaped in secret. Then my poor mother began to pray and weep. The wind began to blow, our sails filled and soon we could no longer see that shore where next morning my mother, insane with sorrow, poured out her cries and wails into Your ears — without Your heed, for You had exploited the attraction of passions in order to kill my own passions, and the too earthly regrets of my mother received their just chastisement by the lash of pain.

St Augustine.

Votive stele. ▸
Open-air museum, Carthage.

Mackerel fishing

When mackerel arrive in a crowded shoal of a metallic blue blending with sea lights, — an immobile mass, the school is caught in a huge net and will fill enormous vats and jars. The fish yield their humors, and their crushed flesh decomposes into a thick, salty brine...

Manilius*.

* A Latin poet of Carthage, Ist century A. D.

Fishing boats on Hammamet beach.

Roman mosaic. Fishing scene.
Bardo Museum.

Trust your boat to the winds...

Trust your boat to the winds but never trust your heart to a woman; a wave is ever surer than a woman's faithfulness. No woman is good, or — if there happens to be one somewhere, I cannot explain how a bad thing ever became good.

Pentadius*.

* Latin poet of Africa, IIIrd century.

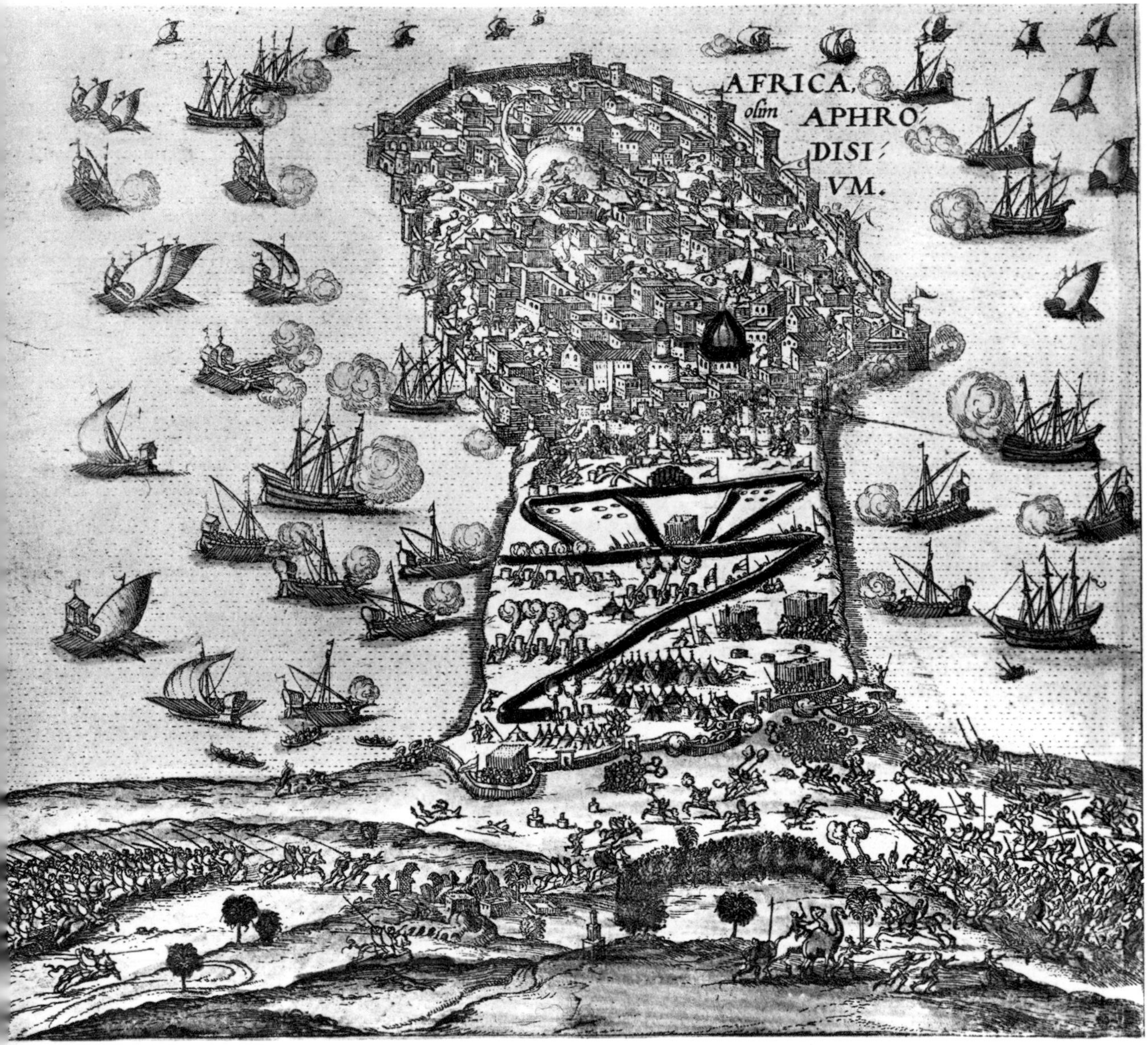

Spanish siege of Mahedia, 1550.

The city of Africa

The city of Africa* is built on a promontory of medium height, and at that time a double wall embraced the entire length of this abrupt point; the outer wall measured five thousand, three hundred and forty Spanish paces, more than half a league around, with a big tower every thirty paces. Moreover, the site was protected by other jutting fortifications: Moors, Turks, and Christians all considered this fortress unconquerable.

Sandoval.

* Africa was the name Europeans still gave Mahedia in the XVIth century.

Mahedia peninsula.

The island of Tabarka

The island of Tabarka lies opposite ancient Tabraca, within firing distance of land. It is almost triangular with a circumference of about a mile or a third of a league. On it rises a mountain which is very steep on the north side, with an easier slope on its south — or land side; on the summit is a very well built castle. The north side is on the edge of a high, steep, inaccessible rock. To the west is a tower and a keep with four bronze cannon bearing the arms of Messers Lomellini of Genoa*.

J.-A. Peyssonnel.

* In the XVIth century the Lomellini of Genoa obtained from the Turks the coral fishing concession at Tabarka.

Tabarka, the needles, the island and the Genoese fort. XVIth century.

The dolphin of Hippo

At Hippo* the pleasures of fishing, boating and swimming delight all ages, but the children do more than anyone else, since they have leisure and the attraction of games is so strong for them. They put their hearts and pride into the game of swimming out to the open sea and the honors fall to the one who goes beyond his companions and farthest from the shore. One day a child, braver than the others, who had gone farther than they — way out, met a dolphin. The dolphin did not dive and flash away but swam ahead, then behind, the boy and turned around him, took the boy on his back, then plunged him in the water again. Afterwards he picked him up and carried the terrified child to the open sea but finally brought him back to the shore and at last returned him to terra firma and his friends. The story spread through the colony, people came from everywhere, the child was considered a prodigy, everyone questioned him ceaselessly, listened to him and told his wonderful tale again and again.

Pliny the Younger.

* This is Hippo Diarrhytos, today called Bizerta.

Roman mosaic.
Cupid riding a dolphin.
Underground villa at Bulla Regia.

The founding of Carthage

Elissa, who had been carried to the shores of Africa, wished to make friends with the inhabitants who were always pleased to have foreigners come and to bargain for goods with them. Then Elissa bought as much land as an ox skin could cover, in order to let her companions rest after their tiring voyage until her departure. She had the hide cut into very narrow strips and thus acquired more land than she had seemed to request. That is why the site since then has been called Byrsa. Hopes for profits attracted the neighbors in crowds around these foreigners to sell them all sorts of produce, and on that account they stayed in the vicinity — finally forming a kind of town. Delegates from Utica brought them gifts saying they were kin and urged them to build a city on this site which destiny had offered them.

Justinian.

Bust of a female satyr.
Undersea diggings at Mahedia.
Bardo Museum.

A view of Carthage from Byrsa hill. Between the blocks of a thick wall, the harbor of the great Punic and Roman city.

Fisherman mending his nets on the shore of Porto Farina.

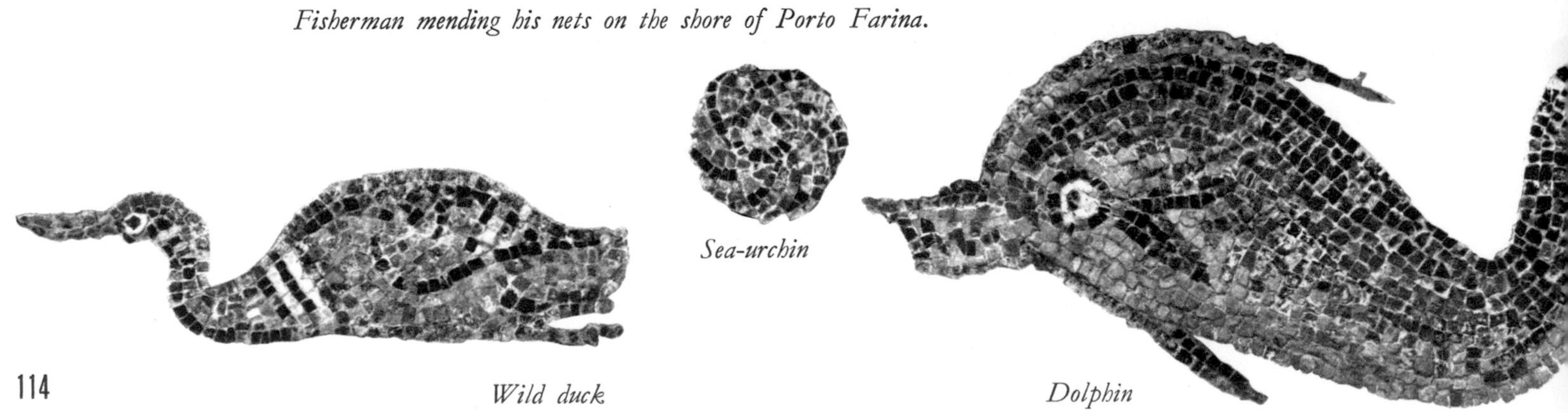

Sea-urchin

Wild duck

Dolphin

The djnoun of the sea

The djnoun of the sea, the *djnoun-al-bahar*, inhabit all oceans, the most powerful dwell in the deepest waters, at the seventh level of depth. They live in marvelous palaces of precious materials, diamonds and rare stones; in the midst of gardens where plants and submarine flowers are in rich bloom, they frolic in the seaweed among fish and shellfish. They are allies of *solt'ân-al-hout*, the powerful lord of sea animals and fish. They have human heads and torsos but from the waist down have fish bodies. The *djinnïate* are very beautiful; they have white skin and long black hair; and when they have nothing to do in their palaces they come up to the surface. They love men very much and hold out their arms to them with plaintive cries. The sailors who see them take them for women in distress and dive into the water. The *djinnïate* hold them in tight embrace to take them to their palaces and overwhelm them with gifts, but the men drown and the *djinnïate* are infinitely sad.

M.L. Dubouloz-Laffin.

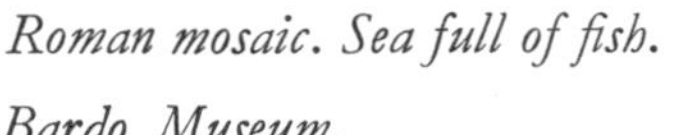

Roman mosaic. Sea full of fish.
Bardo Museum.

Squid

Saw-fish

Eel

Pages 116/117: *Mahedia, fishing port.* ▸

Tunisian Riddles

If it falls who can rebuild it?
If it is angry who can appease it?
The sky is its head, the stars its eyes. The sea.

Tuna fish cannery at Sidi Daoud, Cap Bon.

Our blue lake is covered with flowers.
Two young girls one by one are always crossing it.

The firmament.

Aghlabid reservoirs at Kairouan. Work of the sovereign Abou-Ibrâhîm Ahmed. IXth century.

A builder emir

Huge constructions in different parts of Ifrikiya still preserve the memory of Abou-Ibrâhîm*. The Old Castle cistern was the last of his achievements. Just when it was being finished, he fell ill and every day he asked if the rainwater had begun to fill it. At last they told him there was some water, he was overjoyed and had them bring a cup brimful which he drank enthusiastically, " Praise be to God! " he said, " I could live to see this built. " Soon after he died. The people of Qaîrawân and everyone who visits the city never cease to implore divine mercy for the creator of this useful monument.

En-Noweirî.

* Abou-Ibrâhîm Ahmed, sixth sovereign of the Aghlabid dynasty (856-863).

Great dam of Ben Metir,
which supplies Tunis with potable water.

The new university of Tunis overlooks the workers' section of Melassina.

Tunis, a city of culture

If I had not come to Tunis I would have said that science had left no trace in the West, and that the very name of knowledge had been forgotten, but the Lord of the Universe did not wish that any place on earth be devoid of men skilled in all things. Thus, in this city, I found a representative of each science and people quenching their thirsts at all the tributaries of human knowledge. Professors and students, this cluster of learned men was shining with the most glorious brilliance.

El Abderi.

Divine Muse of Africa

What better or more certain title for praise than the celebration of Carthage where every citizen is a cultivated person and where all devote themselves to all fields of knowledge, children by learning them, young men by showing them off, and old men by teaching them? Carthage, venerable mistress of our province, Carthage, divine Muse of Africa, Carthage, prophetess of the nation which wears the toga...

Apuleius.

A scribe writing. ▶
Christian tumular mosaic.
Bardo Museum.

Tunisian women, the new citizens, taking part in presidential and legislative elections. ▶

A long and delicate task

Should we force women's freedom? No! We have not wanted, and we would never want, to resort to violent measures to force women to go about the streets or to give up their veils. We must make it possible for women to evolve gradually by a patient effort to persuade both men and women, without any direct attack on deeply rooted traditions. Moreover, a sudden breach in our customs and habits could be dangerous. Girls and women without instruction or preparation who might, from one day to the next, become free, could be utterly lost. This development must take place naturally, step by step. Look around you ! Over the last few years a considerable distance has been covered. But there are landmarks we have not yet reached. You may be confident: we shall reach them, and more quickly than we realize. It is in the genius of our nation and the spirit of our revolution to do everything with a minimum of violence or force and instead, with unsparing efforts of conviction and education. The task to be accomplished is long and delicate, but we can accomplish it.*

Habib Bourguiba.

* Taken from the original record of an interview for a women's publication.

The will to live

If one day a nation wishes to live,
Destiny must answer,
Night vanish,
The chains break.

Abou-l-Qâsim Chabbi.

Charter of the Destour Party

Habib Bourguiba speaking to his people.

The Tunisian Liberal Constitutionalist party met at a National Congress May 12 and 13, 1933.

After study of the political activity of the party during the thirteen years since its foundation,

In view of the fact that what was called a policy of collaboration met total failure in this country, also of the fact that the world political and economic situation at present, as well as the present evolution of relationships between nations possessing colonies, and colonized peoples, sets forth the colonial problem in a new light,

In view of that fact economic subordination has led to the ruin of colonized peoples,

In view of the above circumstances and in order to reply to the country's wish, the mission of the Tunisian Liberal Constitutionalist party is to engage the Tunisian people on the path to an emancipation which has become increasingly inevitable.

Thus it is proclaimed that the goal it sets for its political action is to obtain freedom for the Tunisian nation and to endow the country with a stable and inalienable statute by means of a constitution safeguarding Tunisian identity and consecrating national sovereignty by — a Tunisian parliament which, elected by universal suffrage, sets its own program with full legislative powers, and a government responsible to this parliament. Separation of the legislative, executive and judiciary powers. Tunisian justice available to all residents of Tunisian territory. Public freedoms available to all and every Tunisian without discrimination. Compulsory education for all. Protection of the economic life of the country. And, in general, everything which may help bring this country out of its present material ruin and obtain for Tunisia her place in the concert of civilized nations, masters of their fate.

◄ *Aerial view of Tunis and the harbor.*

A widespread burnous

The Arabs compare Tunis to a widespread burnous, and the comparison is accurate. The city opens out in the plain, lightly raised by rolling ground which here and there sets in relief the edges of this large patch of pale houses with high mosque domes and tall minaret towers. One can hardly see or even imagine that there are houses, as this white mass is so compact, dense and low. Around it are three lakes, gleaming under the stubborn sun of the Orient, like plates of steel: far to the north, Sebkha-er-Riana; to the west, Sebkha-Sedjoumi visible beyond the city; southward, the great lake, Bahira or Lake of Tunis; and to the north again, the sea, a deep gulf, also like a lake in its distant frame of mountains. On a brilliant sunny day, the sight of this city among its lakes lying in this landscape enclosed by far away mountains — of which the highest, Zaghouan, appears almost always cloud-topped in winter — this is the most striking landscape and probably the most charming which exists on the edge of the continent of Africa.

Guy de Maupassant.

From Carthage to Tomorrow

In the same way as one tries to interpret a face, one also attempts to give a soul to the map of a country. We no longer limit ourselves to the mere knowledge of its position, its boundaries, or where the mountains, plains and rivers are situated, but we want to find out about the major events in its history and the character of the men who people it. I dream of a picture that was the Libya of the Phoenicians, the Africa of the Romans, Ifrikiya for the Arabs and the Principality of Tunis for the Turks. It seems to me that the merchants of Tyre must have brought their goods to this uneven coastline; that Carthage, at the meeting of the two Mediterranean basins, was to become the metropolis of a vast empire; that Rome would destroy her dangerous rival, and subdue without difficulty this land so open and easy to penetrate; that the Arabs must also in their turn conquer her to Islamize and Arabize her; that the Turks must also become her masters for the purpose of increasing their pirate hideouts; that Europe, so near, would end by extending her sway over her. Today, Tunis has freed herself, and in the spirit of her élite, concerned with her continuity yet eager for modernism, I discover more hidden relationships with the profile of this part of Africa, turned towards another continent, and halfway between the Orient and the Occident. But quickly, I change my mind, I understand that I am deluding myself and allowing myself to be seduced by a naive determinism or an empty metaphor. One can make maps say everything if one knows how to make them speak, faces deceive us despite the science of Lavater and Gall. But first this calls for a simple lesson in geography.

1. The earth and the days

Arabian geographists have called North Africa 'jazîrat al maghreb': island of the sunset. An island? It is bordered by the sea on the west, the north and the east, and in the south by the Sahara. Of the three countries of which it is made up, Tunisia is the smallest and the most easterly. But in describing it, we will reverse the usual procedure, and start in the south and come up to the north.

First there is the desert, with its rocky table-land and sand dunes, which stretch way out of sight. Owing to lack of rain, the average annual rainfall is hardly 100 millimeters, only xerophyte plants grow here, which camels, sheep and goats are able to eat. A fractional part of the nomadic tribes, living in tents, travel through these desolate stretches. Here on the edge of the great 'chotts' the water that has risen from the depths of the earth has created the beautiful oases of Djerid-Toser, Nefta, El Oudiane — and of Nefzaoua, Kebili and Douz — islets of non-migratory life where, on a few hundred acres, plantations of date palms are clustered, in whose shade fruit trees and vegetables are cultivated. However, the South is not confined to the monotony of the desert, broken at long intervals by the flowing life of an oasis. In the Matmata mountain chain, less frugally watered — because of its height — small stone embankments are enough in the ravines and valleys to hold back the water and the earth. Palm, olive and fig trees add to the meager resources of cattle breeding. Along the shore spreads a large plain where the rainfall is heavier due to the sea nearby. Here too, one finds oases, such as Gabès and El Hamma; where cereals can be cultivated, but with a poor and uncertain yield; owing to better spaced plantations, olive trees grow well in the Sarsis region. Djerba, as an island, has a special climate, and is planted with palm and olive trees, and divided into innumerable gay gardens. In the shallows along the coastline, a valuable contribution is made by fishing, especially, for sponges.

North of the Gafsa mountain chain — where at the end of the last century important veins of lime phosphate were discovered — the Steppes begin. They have an average rainfall of 200 to 400 millimeters, but this varies drastically from year to year. In the High Steppes, at the foot of the mountains covered with Aleppo pine forests, spread vast alfa grass fields. The pulling up of these grasses, which are raw material for the esparto factories and the big paper manufacturers, assures seasonal work for the semi-nomadic population who otherwise live off hazardous cereal cultivation and the breeding of sheep and goats condemned to a constant change of feeding grounds.

In the east come the Low Steppes, with their gloomy plains, dominated here and there by small heights and crossed from time to time by ' oueds ' which flood the Kairouan plain. Here also the population is semi-nomadic — spending part of the year in stone houses, the rest in tents, and living from growing cereals and breeding sheep and goats. The cultivation of olive trees is more profitable, it can be developed on the grazing lands and leads to the settling of the tribes as shepherd-farmers. To develop a magnificent forest of olive trees with an abundant harvest in the region of Sfax, it is enough to plant the trees 25 meters apart so that their roots can draw upon sufficient earth. These new plantations contrast with the old ones of Sahel, and one admires the way in which they are regularly planted. The country of gentle hills along the borders of the shore, around Susa, being more northerly, profits from a heavier rainfall. The trees are thicker but the yield less. The cultivation of vegetable oils assures a relatively easier living for the sedentary population thickly grouped in villages and small market towns. Along all the eastern coast where the olive is king, oil refineries and soap factories have been established. Yet this does not stop the sea's richness from being turned to advantage: fishing fleets from Susa and Mahedia are specialized in fishing sardines and anchovies for the many tinning factories. Along the coastline, where evaporation is very high, salt fields are being started (Sfax, Monastir).

Beyond the long mountain chain running southwest-northeast called the Great Dorsal ending at Kef Chambi at 1,543 meters, the Tell starts. Here the soil is more fertile and the rainfall heavier and more regular — an average of 400 to 600 millimeters yearly. The ' oueds ' are much larger and permit the building of dams for irrigation and electric power, and the population has been able to settle on the land. In the west, the high Tell becomes hilly country covered with Aleppo pine forests and valleys favorable to the cultivation of cereals (barley and wheat) and the breeding of cattle (goats, sheep and cows). Around Kef, the subsoil conceals veins of phosphate (Kalâa Djerda), of iron (Djerissa) and of lead and zinc (Sidi Amor). The north of the Tell is more varied. The Khroumir mountain group which gets more than 800 millimeters of rain yearly, is covered with beautiful forests of cork oak. The Medjerda valley, the main water source, was already celebrated in ancient times for its rich wheat fields (Souk el Arba, Souk el Khemis, Béjà). Plentiful pasture land assures a high return in cattle breeding. Today, mines of iron (Douaria, Tamera), lead and zinc (Djebel Hallouf, Djebel Semen, Sidi bou Aouane, El Greffa) are being exploited. To the east the lower Tell, the plains of Tunis and Cap Bon peninsula, all lend themselves with success to very varied cultivation: cereals (Zaghouan), olive groves (Tébourba), grapes (Grombalia), citrus fruit (Menzel bou Zelfa and Hammamet), spices and herbs (Nabel) and everywhere there are truck gardens irrigated by wells. There has always been fishing in the Gulf of Tunis, and the tuna nets stop the shoals of tuna that spawn all along the coastline (Sidi Daoud). Finally, we must mention the many stone and clay quarries. These varied resources, in addition to those of the hinterland, furnish many important materials to industry — which, however, has to import its fuel (the coal from Cap Bon is mediocre and so far no oil has been found). Thus Tunis has been able to become an industrial center (flour-mills, distilleries, canning factories, factories for building materials).

Coming up from the south to the north, the Tell appears to be a happy Tunisia.

From the Sahara to the sea, the landscape is very varied, green oases in the middle of the desert sand, steppes where the herds graze, forests of cork oak, olive groves, grain fields, truck gardens, citrus fruit orchards, hillsides covered with vines, all cradled in the rhythm of the seasons, which peasant folklore vividly expresses.

The great September storms, which plentifully water the thirsty earth after the heat of summer, announce the fall. The air is fresher, but the weather remains mild (the average fall temperature in Tunis is $15\frac{1}{2}^{\circ}$ C. with extreme averages of 25.1° to 6.8°). This is the time when the pomegranate ripens: " Big as a fist, it holds a hundred and a thousand "; in the southern palm plantations, date picking starts; " Our red cow has a collar around its neck, her meat would sell in every market, but she stays tied up in her stable ". In the Khroumir forests concentrated around Tabarka, the first layer of cork is cut from the trees. The " fellahs " of the Tell have hailed the first rains with joy, " Autumn rain, fertility ". They work hard and hurry to start sowing, " he who does not sow early will never build a stack ". But the semi-nomads coming down again towards the steppes with their herds, have often to wait a long time for the needed heavy showers, " In the north, there are seven clouds that give rain, here there is only one ". If the drought continues, they cry out for divine mercy, and long lines of children go about the country singing, " Our fathers who are grown up have been unjust and violent, but we, we are little. Be clement towards us, oh thou who forgiveth. " Meanwhile in the Sahel and in the Sfaxian forest, there is harvest fever. " A negress, perched on high, cries, 'Oh, my happiness, Oh, my beauty' ": it is the black olive, on the tree, that attracts attention and excites envy. Standing on ladders, with horn on their fingers, the men and women knock down the fruit, swollen with juice, on to sheets spread on the ground. Day and night, the carts carry their loads to the oil refineries, where the grindstones turn ceaselessly and the oil for the coming year flows from the presses.

With winter, the temperature drops. (The winter average at Tunis is 11.6° C. with extreme averages from 18.1° to 6.4°.) There are many sunny days, but it rains one day out of three, and sometimes the mountain tops are covered with snow. " It is the money that comes from the mountain of pearls, no workman ever minted it and it never entered any workshop. " If the mistral blows and the sea rises, the sailing boats and trawlers cannot leave the ports. In the steppes it is the slack season, which coincides with the pulling up of the alfa grass. In the Sahel and the Sfaxian forest, the olive harvest continues, after which the trees must be pruned and the soil tilled. In the orchards of Cap Bon, the orange trees are bowed down under the weight of the fruit, " By God, people are surprising, they throw away gold, and eat silver " ! The fall rains have made sowing possible, but it is the winter rains that decide the harvest, "Water the seed, I will show you a marvel ". Every shower is welcomed like a blessing: " Khir Allah, rahmat Allah: the gift of God and his divine mercy ". And in the gardens, the seedlings are being prepared for spring cultivation.

" Who was always in the frost and cold and came out one fine day in splendid finery? " In these two verses, the peasant could express his feelings before nature's awakening in the spring. The weather grows milder. (The spring average in Tunis is 19.2° C. with extreme averages of 29.° and 10.3°.) The herds find plentiful grass in the fresh green fields. "In April, the shoots come up, even at the bottom of the wells." While waiting for the cereal harvest — which also needs the spring rains — the young sheep are weaned and sheep shearing begins: " A pretty girl with her hair well arranged, has shaken her coat, then got up again, after submitting to the skilled shears, " it is the sheep, naked from the shearer's scissors. In the oases, an incision in the palm trees makes the "lagmi" run, which ferments and intoxicates like wine. On the shores of Cap Bon, tuna fish are caught in the chambers of the dead, and off Sahel, the sea glitters at night with a thousand lights from the fishermen fishing with lanterns. Before spring draws to a close, the semi-nomads from the center harvest their wheat and barley, often poor, and leave their dried up steppes to drive their herds to the perennial pasture lands of the Tell, and to hire themselves out for a later but more abundant and steady harvest.

Now it is summer and it grows hotter (the average Tunis summer temperature is 25.6° C. with extreme averages of 32.6° and 18.7°). Beware of the sirocco which brings deep into the Tell the burning desert winds ! On big modern plantations, the role of man is limited to that of driving machines, but in fields belonging to the poor or average ' fellahs ', the oldest traditions survive. The harvesters move forward in line, cutting the ears with their sickles, and setting down behind them the bound-up sheaves. The cereal is then carried to the threshing floor to be beaten and sifted by the stamping of horses' hooves or the roundabout of the ' jarroucha ', a sort of sledge with flint spikes like, the ancient ' tribulum '. " A wooden plate playing over gold. " Then, to separate the grain from the straw, it is turned on the threshing floor with forks while the wind blows, " Give us a breeze, Oh Lord, send down to us your favor, Oh God, give us a wind from the east, favorable and beneficial ". The grain is hardly reaped when grape harvesting begins. " Female climbing over the ground, her son is a sultan, her grandson a Satan, " such is the vine whose fruit is delicious, but the drink drawn from it is forbidden by the Koran. It is in the heart of summer that the water-melons are picked, " Our cupola is green, its inhabitants are black. The hand of God closes it and iron opens it. " The red peppers, " redder than I, redder than thou, redder than a drop of blood, guess what it is or go away ". Grape harvesting continues until fall. Thus the eternal cycle, bearing away the earth and the days, is renewed.

2. *Changing Civilizations*

" Such are the days, we give them to nations each in turn. " This verse from the Koran is haunting if one undertakes to call up the history of this land in the heart of the Mediterranean, prey to successive invaders who, one after the other, have left the imprint of their civilizations.

Even prehistoric times had their invasions. The Atérians of whom some scanty remains have been found in the sediment of the Akarit 'oued' and the stones of Ain Meterchem must have been overwhelmed and obliterated by men — from where — who implanted the Capsian civilization in the country. These conquerors, whose physical type is related to the Cro-Magnon, and who lived from crops and hunting did well in cut stone, but they did not know how to invent polished stone, nor how to cultivate the soil or breed animals. It was foreigners who taught them, before submerging them. All this plays, no doubt, an essential role in the formation of the ethnic complex which made up, at the dawn of history, the native population of the country: the Berbers. This people showed in ancient times true unity and, in spite of the many influences on them over the course of centuries, they succeeded in keeping more than one element of their original personality. The Berbers spoke similar dialects, sharing the Libyan tongue from which the present Berber language is derived (widespread in Algeria and Morocco, much less in Tunisia).

They were, above all, cattle breeders, wandering the whole year with their herds and living necessarily in mobile dwellings, the *mapalia*, which Sallust compares to ships' hulls; yet all the same they farmed and some settled on the land, their stone huts grouped in villages on steep sites. The needs of a pastoral or agricultural life led the patriarchal families to gather in much larger units, tribes of farmers and shepherds, in constant conflict. The gathering of the elders, doubtless very like the *miyâd*, which survived in Tunisia until recently, took all decisions of collective interest and in wartime appointed the chief who would lead the tribe in battle. If the tribes united and placed themselves under the command of an *aguellid* or king, a more or less durable kingdom was formed. The Berbers had no written literature (they were late in adopting an alphabet); their art in which geometric drawings prevailed over imitation of nature, remained rough; their animist religion fell back on the belief in an infinity of spirits and by the use of magical practices, one could be assured of their help and could check the power of evil spells. (The popularity of *jnûn* and the cult of saints, still very much alive, are of Berber origin.) Called either Libyans or Numidians, the Berbers named themselves *Imazighen*, " free men ". In fact, all through the ages they have never ceased to prove their spirit of lively independence — all the more so as history has never ceased giving them masters.

Carthage, traditionally founded in 814 B.C. by the runaway Elissa-Dido, was not the first place to be created by the Phoenicians on the east Berber coast; Utica, Hippo Diarrhytos and Hadrumetum are three centuries older — but it was going to eclipse its elders with its feats and power. At first only an ordinary colony recognizing the sovereignty of Tyre, it soon became the base for new Phoenician expansion in the western Mediterranean basin, founding in its turn colonies on the coast of Africa, the Balearics, Corsica, Sardinia and Sicily which it disputed with Greece. Carthage, originally a foreign enclave having to pay tribute for the soil it lived on, conquered the Medjerda valley, Cap Bon and the Sahel, submitted the Berbers to its domination, crushed them with taxes, and ruthlessly suppressed their revolts. And after reasserting its pre-eminence over the early Phoenician colonies, it became in the IVth century — which saw the destruction of Tyre by Alexander — the uncontested capital of a great empire, under an oligarchy. The Carthaginians had an unequaled knowledge of the sea routes and the expeditions of Hannon and Himilcon explored the Atlantic coast of Africa as far as Cameroon and Europe as far as Brittany, developing new fields of action which they tried to keep secret. Their ships, for years the best, plowed the seas of the old world; their merchants made their way into every country of which they had learned to speak the language: *Omnias linguas scit,* one says of *Poenulus* in Plautus; they bought here to re-sell there, profiting by every deal. In their holds they transported oil from Sicily, wine from Rhodes, salt provisions from Syrtis, gold from Sudan, tin from Britain, silver from Spain, iron from Elba, fabrics from Malta, Egyptian glass, Greek ceramics, as well as all the produce of the Carthaginian workshops and the subject hinterlands, silverware, jewelry, materials, leather and pottery.

On landowners' domains skillful technical cultivation was introduced for wheat, olive trees and vines, and the Romans later made much of Magon's agricultural science. Polybius declares that Carthage, at one time, was the richest town in the world. Of its civilization its religion is best known, with its great gods Baal Hammon and Tanit, who demanded human sacrifice. (One can no longer doubt the truth of classical reports, Diodorus of Sicily among others, since excavations have produced thousands of urns containing charred bones of children which were found in the town's most ancient sanctuary near the old ports.) Apparently the Carthaginians created nothing original in art or thought, but they were not unresponsive to Greek genius. Recent works devoted to the Punic world emphasize its profound Hellenization from the Vth century B.C. on. Flaubert's *Salammbô* has revived Hannibal's city in the image of a " mysterious Jerusalem ", and one knows today that " it was very similar to the Greek towns of Sicily which its ships visited ". The sailors and merchants from Tyre mixed their blood with the Berbers, so that some towns were, they say, peopled by Libyphoenicians and the influence of Punic civilization was thus stronger on the natives of the Carthaginian state — subject with time to a less harsh domination. By degrees it won over the Berber realms which had succeeded in keeping their independence. Massinissa, the prince of the Massylii, whose power spread over part of the Tunisian Tell, made his people adopt the methods of cultivation, the industrial techniques, the customs and the religion of the Punics, and made their language official. The Semitization of the Berbers was halted by the Romans, who, after three long wars, destroyed the power of Carthage in 146 B.C. and quickly subdued the whole country in spite of Jugurtha's desperate action.

Rome, in the first century before our era, united the ancient territory of Carthage with part of the Massylian realm, and made one province out of it, the province of Africa, which corresponds almost exactly to the Tunisia of today. When by the command of Augustus, Dido's city, described in Virgil's *Aeneid,* was restored, it became the capital and the seat of the Roman proconsul. A public register of land was made of the province, — traces are still left, and it was opened up for colonization. In the shelter of the *limes* erected on the Saharian borders, and with peace assured by the legions, roads and hydraulic installations helped travel and the development of the land. The cultivation of cereals made great progress, supplied stocks, as did the olive groves which in the central steppes absorbed some of the land abandoned to the wandering herds. With economic prosperity came an extraordinary expansion of town life: one can still admire the orderly planning of the Roman towns, the amphitheatre at El Djem, the theater at Dougga, the forum at Thuburbo Majus, the thermal baths of Antoninus in Carthage, fed by a colossal aqueduct, and everywhere rich dwellings with mosaic paving, here the Hellenic civilization triumphed, which Rome made known to all the world. Romanization meant the spreading of a language, witness the thousands of inscriptions carved in stone; the birth of a literature, of which Apuleius, the charming story teller of *The Golden Ass* and the subtle rhetorician of *Floridae*, is the most remarkable representative. Finally, the introduction of a religion in which the cult of the Emperor was allied to that of the gods who protected him and who, in connection with the oldest beliefs, gave birth to striking syncretisms: Baal Hammon being identified with Saturn and Tanit with Juno. Then when, in the synagogues of the Jewish colonies, the Good Word was preached, Christianity spread, and Tertullian, who was born in Carthage, wrote the first *Apologetica*. First exposed to ruthless persecution, the new religion, due to the faith of its martyrs on African soil, as in the whole Empire, asserted itself and in the end was raised to the position of State religion: all the Roman towns in Africa had their bishops and churches of which traces remain. The Berbers, who, in the first century of our era, rose against Rome at the call of Tacfarinas, ended by following the new order. A middle class of land owners was formed, became Latinized, obtained civic freedom and at last saw themselves granted political rights equal to those of Roman citizens. But, from the third century on, the dangerous state of a world founded on slavery suddenly worsened. The peace of the countryside was troubled by peasant and proletarian unrest, the Berbers' poverty contrasted with the luxury and richness of a Romanized aristocracy. It is not surprising that they rose against their unjust fate under the banner of donatist heresy, which St. Augustine opposed, " God is their only refuge.

At times, in the bitterness of their suffering, they cannot help wishing for the arrival of the Barbarians, " wrote Salvian. When the Barbarians came to Africa, — Vandals led by Genséric — they had no trouble in conquering, in 439, a country undermined from within. These invaders have been given an unmerited reputation: they destroyed little and seem rather to have kept, during one century, the Roman civilization which pleased them, and to have relieved the exploitation of the rural peoples. However, they could not stop the Berbers, established in the steppes of the province, from accentuating their pressure and crossing the boundaries. The Byzantines, who, under Justinian, reconquered Africa from the Vandals in 533, and restored the old order, gave the country renewed prosperity; but in spite of the formidable fortresses they built with stones from Roman monuments, they failed to enforce the frontiers of an impoverished territory. And although they reduced the Berber revolts, they could not stand up to new enemies from the East, the Arabs, who launched their first assault in 647 on the ancient Sufetula countryside.

The Arabs settled in the country, founding the town of Kairouan in 670 at the command of 'Uqba ibn Nâfi', driving out the last Byzantine garrisons of Carthage in 698, overcoming the Berber resistance instigated by the Kahena, and achieved early in the VIIIth century the conquest of North Africa. But the subject Berbers quickly split into separate states — all unification was precarious and short-lived. In the East, Ifrikiya, whose name reminds one of Roman Africa, was first administered by governors under the orders of the caliphs of Damascus and Baghdad. In the year 800, the Arab emir Ibn al-Aghlab founded a dynasty of which the princes reigned at Kairouan as independent sovereigns. A Berber tribe, which had been won over to the chi'ite heresy, brought to power in 909 the prince, 'Ubayd Allah, who took the title of Caliph and founded the dynasty of the Fatimides, and made Mahedia his capital. When, in 973, the fourth dynasty decided, after having conquered Egypt, to move the seat of the caliphate to Cairo, he asked one of his vassals to govern Ifrikiya in his name; the Berber Bologgîn ben Zîrî passed on his power to his descendants. But towards the middle of the XIth century, a Zeirid prince renounced the chi'ite heresy and the Fatimide sovereignty. To punish him for his rebellion, the caliph of Cairo let loose on the eastern Berbers fierce Arab tribes from the Delta, the Banû Hillal. Their invasion in 1050 initiated a period of troubles and anarchy; the country cut itself up into little rival principalities, and in 1135 the Normans from Sicily took possession of the coast towns. The Almohad, 'Abd al-Mumîn, after taking over Morocco, crossed the central Maghreb, penetrated into Ifrikiya, and entered Tunis in 1159 as a conqueror, subduing all North Africa to one state. But in 1228, Abû Zakâriya, who governed Ifrikiya in the name of the Almohads, asserted his independence and founded the dynasty of the Hafsids who made Tunis their capital and reigned over three centuries, to modern times. The Arab conquest had opened a new period in the country's history. The Berbers, converted to Islam, apostatized more than once, asserting their particularism by enthusiastically embracing heretical doctrines but ended by being completely won over to Moslem orthodoxy. (Except for the Almohad period, the Jewish and Christian minorities, subject to the statute of the *dhimmis*, were treated with tolerance.) An Arab population more numerous in the East than the rest of Maghreb (especially after the ethnic additions of the XIth century), aided the mixing of races, and the language of the Prophet replaced Berber and Latin. A new economy took root, in the country a type of feudalism was set up, in the towns the first corporations of skilled workmen and merchants were formed, controlled by the *hisba* and grouped in 'souks'. Prosperity reigned at first but waned after the Hilalian invasion; however, when a strong power under the Hafsids was restored, an undeniable rebirth took place. Witness to the medieval Ifrikiyan civilization are the Aghlabid hydraulic works, the great mosques of Kairouan, Tunis and Mahedia, a whole architecture subjected to Oriental or Hispano-Moorish influences. The towns, and especially the capitals, became brilliant centers of culture where medieval Islamic science and letters blossomed. Lawyers, such as Suhnûn and Ibn Abî Zayd, doctors of medicine, such as Ibn Jazzâr and Ishâq ben Sulaymân Israelî — whose works were made known to the Occident by the Latin translations of Constantine the African — poets, such as Ibn Charaf and Ibn Hanî, and finally, the historian of *Kitâb al-'Ibâr,* Ibn Khaldûn, the philosopher of the *Prolegomenes,* are the great names. At the end of the Middle Ages there was stagnation in every field, — production techniques, social structure, thought and art, as though Arab civilization, whose influence on Europe had been both profound and happy, was now out of breath.

After a long duel with the Spanish, who, with Charles V at their head, took Tunis in 1535 and attempted numerous expeditions (against Mahedia and Djerba among others), to stop their expansion, the Turks succeeded in taking Ifrikiya in 1574, and turning it into a province of the Ottoman Empire. The power, at first divided among the pacha, the dey and the bey, ended by coming under one bey. Hussein ben Ali changed the regime into an hereditary monarchy in favor of the dynasty he founded in 1705, and the sovereignty of the Sublime Porte in this remote land was to become only nominal. The Turks were much occupied with piracy, and this brought ships, cargoes and captives to Tunisian ports. This predatory activity supplied profits in prizes, made high ransom money from those who were 'redeemed', and also provided workmen for the arsenals, and gangs who rowed the galleys, as well as the *râis* who commanded them, ex-slaves who, renouncing their faith, became "national Turks", (Issouf Raîs was English and Osta Morat, Genoese). The role of the Moors, without doubt less romantic, seems to have been more fruitful; chased out of Spain at the beginning of the XVIIth century, they found refuge in Tunisia. The Andalusians made beautiful, cleverly irrigated gardens in the Tell countryside, and in Tunis developed the manufacture of the 'chéchia', silk weaving and the art of glazed ceramics. The Jews, descendants of the Marrans, whom the Inquisition had forced to flee and who had settled in Leghorn, started coming in during the XVIIth century to increase the population of the capital; they introduced new commercial techniques and at the same time created small European trading colonies. However, it did not seem that the country's economy or culture had been seriously changed by the Turkish conquest. The Levantines who settled in the country were never very numerous: their language, limited to small circles, had little effect on Arabic. They were of the orthodox Moslem religion: neither the beliefs nor the observances of the population were affected. Although the architecture of the period has an original style (the charming Turkish and Husseinite mosques of Tunis are easily recognizable by their octagonal minarets), it is still Islamic art. As to letters and science, they continued in the traditions inherited from the Arab Middle Ages, with a decline which became more and more evident. Is this sufficient to permit one to speak of a change in the succession of civilizations?

3. *The calm of the Orient*

"At present, Islam, driven back to Asia and Africa, and tolerated only in a corner of Europe, owing to the jealousy of the Christian powers, has long since deserted the realm of world history and returned to the indifference and the calm of the Orient." Thus, some hundred and fifty years ago, Hegel concluded the work that he had devoted to the expansion of Mohammedanism in his *Lesssons on the Philosophy of History.* His judgment was severe, but he found his justification in the extreme decadence into which the Islamic States had fallen, after the former brilliance and power of their weapons, the prosperity of their economy and the grandeur of their civilization.

The result being, that at the beginning of the last century, Tunisia did not escape the common destiny of the Moslem world, which had scarcely changed since the Middle Ages. In the country, there were some islets of small peasant holdings; but over vast stretches, were properties belonging only to the sovereign, great families or religious foundations — *habous* — where farmers and tenant farmers labored in a state of semi-servitude; on the edges were collective lands belonging to shepherd-farmers condemned to a semi-roving life according to the rhythm of the seasons. The legal method of land holding was such that it discouraged tenants from making an effort from which they gained nothing and so they let large fertile regions go to waste; obsolete tools and methods of cultivation were an obstacle to any rational improvement; and, periodically, the return of a dry year would mean a bad harvest, famine and epidemics. Domestic industries, weaving, basket making, pottery, satisfied for the most part the needs of the rural masses. Whatever else they needed they asked for in the town where they went to sell their produce. There, the corporations of skilled workmen were subjected to the *orf*, that most thorough of controls, custom, which transmitted from father to son the same tools and the same gestures to work silk and cotton, leather and wood, copper and silver. The tradespeople, also grouped in corporations, limited their business to internal exchange. Of the non-Moslems, the Europeans of various nationalities and the native Jews had the monopoly of foreign trade. It was no different one or two centuries earlier, except that the show of arms by the great western powers had now ended piracy and slavery. A stagnant economy, —the country was untouched by even a beginning of an industrial revolution,— means an unchanging social structure. The historian may in spite of the lack of documentation at hand, sketch in the hierarchy of conditions. But how could he find class dynamics there, where one generation simply succeeds the other? A sovereign, who nominally recognized Turkish sovereignty, exercised all the powers of an absolute monarch. It was the bey who governed, made laws and rendered justice. He entrusted the highest state responsibilities to freed slaves, the mamelukes : strangers to the country, they were all the more devoted to his person. The caïds, governors, whom he placed at the head of the tribes and the provinces, settled small lawsuits, saw that his orders were executed, and above all helped to collect the taxes which swelled the treasure of the kingdom and of the king. Twice a year, he left, at the head of his army, to collect tribute from his people, and often he met fierce resistance; it would have been hard to succeed if the stubborn ones had got together; but the tribes were all each others' enemies, yesterday conquered by the bey, today helping the bey to conquer. Woe to the conquered, who would have to pay even more than had been asked of them and whose land would be confiscated to become the property of a favorite. Oh well! It is the way of the world. If there is a chance, someone will always help a pretender to mount the throne and then take a discount on his gratitude; internal war devastated the country to bring to power a prince who would reign as did all his predecessors. In the towns, where there survived all that was exquisite which Moslem civilization had created, — the peace of great estates and the murmur of fountains, pleasures without remorse and the love of speech, subtleties of courtesy and contempt of haste — culture was confined mainly to theology, law, grammar and 'belles lettres', and sclerosis had set in. Just what was necessary of astronomy to foretell the phases of the moon and enough arithmetic to settle the fortune of an estate. The Great Mosque-University of Tunis was ignorant of the advance made by the West over the science of the Arabs and the incredible power that they had acquired over Nature. What matter, if one remains faithful to strict orthodoxy and believes as one should believe?

One cannot help but ask oneself the reasons for this inertia. Must one hold Islam responsible? It has been done more than once. It has been observed that the Moslem religion lays too much emphasis on contemplation and turns aside from action; that the dogma of predestination disposes souls to fatalism; that the prohibition by the Koran of loans at interest was not favorable to the development of capitalism; that the abolition of all innovations or *bid'a,* suspected of heresy, resulted necessarily in scientific and technical immobilization. But these features are found in other religions without their having hindered the progress of the peoples who practised them. A life of contemplation had been encouraged by the Gospels, predestination was strongly affirmed by the Protestants (which did not stop them from being in Europe an undeniable ferment of progress); Catholicism had firmly forbidden loans at interest. There is no country where scientific and technical innovations have not had to overcome religious dogma and social conservatism. All religions have had to become more flexible so as to adapt to modern times and new requirements. But should one not explain exactly why Islam was not compelled to reform? Without doubt, cultural rigidity accounted in a large measure for the economic and social rigidity. But is it enough to blame this cultural rigidity on the "Arab mind"? Are there no objective reasons? One thinks of the decline of the Mediterranean after the great discoveries, of the piracy that made possible a flow of riches without having to produce them; the near monopoly of non-Moslems over external exchange which was an obstacle to the formation of commercial capital; the fact that the Islamic world had not known the sudden expansion of markets which had put Europe on the road to industrial capitalism — all factors which probably precluded here the appearance of a modern middle class, which was at the source of the economic, social, political and cultural revolutions in the Occident. But these are only hypotheses; we will not assert ourselves when the wisest men give an example of modesty and prudence. One statement is certain: cultural, economic and social rigidity were both engendered and encouraged in order to maintain in Tunisia, as in the other Islamic countries, a paralyzed civilization.

An anecdote may illustrate the split between a sluggish Orient and a Faustian Occident. When Bonaparte was in Cairo, the French let loose their Montgolfière balloons and were convinced they had impressed the population. An Arab annalist, al-Jabarti, expressed the true sentiments of the Egyptians, "The French made a monster that went up into the sky meaning to reach God and insult him, but it only went up a little way and then fell down, ridiculously powerless." However, that superb tranquillity was quickly replaced among the best minds by agonized searching: whence comes the progress of one world and the stagnation of the other? The increase of contacts between peoples and their increasing wealth of comparisons hastened the flowering of modern ideas in Islam. A thinker, who was also a statesman, upheld the cause of Tunisia in the last century. Khereddine, who had thoroughly visited Europe, published in 1867 an important work entitled, *A most reliable guide to the state of nations*, in which he drew up a table of all the countries for which he had been able to assemble detailed documentation. The preface to the work, the only part to be translated in French, under the title of *Necessary reforms for the Moslem States*, is a coherent program for the restoration of the Islamic

States. The master theme: " Help one another in the intelligent choice of the most efficient methods to improve the state of the Islamic nation, increase and develop the elements of its civilization, widen the circles of science and knowledge, increase public wealth by the development of agriculture, commerce and industry, and to establish first of all, as a basis, a good governmental system from which would come that confidence which produces in its turn perseverance of effort and the gradual improvement of all things, in short, that which exists in Europe today. " It is not possible here to go into details of the developments to which the work is devoted. But, nearly a century later, one still admires the lucidity, the realism and the spirit. Who would not then think the " Europeanization " of Tunisia might have been possible without colonization? But one doubts it, when one sees Khereddine, supported by a weak elite, coming up against the hostility of the ulemas and of official power, calling on Europe. "It would be both just and necessary, " he writes, " if the civilized governments of Europe, who so often boast and rightly so of their love of the good of humanity, would come at last sincerely to the aid of the aspirations of the population and eliminate the obstacles to the introduction and the function of liberal reforms for the Moslems, whom one sees still groaning under the yoke of despotism. " Fatal inconsistency of doctrine? The despair of a misunderstood precursor, who yields too quickly? One can speculate forever on the history that might have been but not affect the history that was.

Tunisia had undertaken the way to reform long before Khereddine had written his book. Under the influence of European powers and particularly of France, who, in 1830, became master of Algeria, the last independent beys, Ahmed, Mohammed and Mohammed es-Sadok, had wanted to modernize the country. The most spectacular acts were, in 1857, the proclamation of a fundamental Pact — a declaration of the rights of man — and, in 1861, the concession of a constitution, which theoretically ended the absolute power of the beys and endowed the state with new institutions. But these reforms, dictated by foreigners whom they served, did not come from a rising, new class and could only be a 'trompe-l'œil', behind which the old system continued. The beys, under the pretext of opening their kingdom to progress, contracted enormous expenses to equip their armies, added the cost of building steam warships and built sumptuous palaces, all of which exhausted the treasury. It was not enough to deplete the state treasury, it was again necessary to get loans from outside; the capital vanished in commissions, bribes and embezzlements by greedy dignitaries, and the arrears continually made public costs heavier. In 1864, the bey decided to double the head tax his subjects were forced to pay. This was the signal for a big popular revolt which now inflamed the whole country. But because of the rebels' hesitation, and their internal differences, on which officialdom knew very well how to play, they were checked. The population was ruthlessly repressed and fined. In the ruined countryside, neglect of cultivation and a drought brought famine and epidemics. The treasury resources continued to fall and it was necessary to face up to the interest on an already increased debt. This was bankruptcy of the State and, in 1869, Tunisian finances were put under the control of an international commission. The bey entrusted Khereddine with the responsibilities of prime minister, and he made, by wise administration, a praiseworthy effort towards economic recovery. But it was an epoch when the great powers shared the world. French, English and Italian business men quarrelled over railway concessions, mining interests, landed property, and European consuls were at their service. In 1878, at the Berlin Congress, in spite of Italian claims, Germany encouraged France to develop her influence in Tunisia, and England let it be known that she would not oppose it.

Khereddine, before being evicted from power, tried in vain to avoid the inevitable by placing Tunisia under the protection of the Sublime Porte. The Khroumir invasions beyond the Algerian-Tunisian frontiers gave to the France of Jules Ferry an opportune pretext to intervene, and, after a rapid expedition, France forced the bey to sign the Treaty of Bardo, in 1881, which established the protectorate. It was to be under foreign tutelage that Tunisia would wrench herself free of the calm of the Orient.

4. *The shock of Europe*

Only in an old colony that has been liberated can one be fair about colonization. Not only because the time of stubborn apologetics and bitter polemics has passed, but moreover because, in a new phase, the objectivity for which one strives is easier. A Tunisian statesman confided to us the other day: " We are now able to talk as calmly about colonization as about other period of our history. "

The protectorate respected the existence of a Tunisian State and the beys of the Husseinite dynasty continued to reign. But the recent agreements obliged them to proceed with all the administrative, legal and financial reforms that the French Government judged necessary, and, soon, a Resident General held in fact all legal and executive powers to govern Tunisia, " in the name of the bey from top to bottom. " Thus a new administration was superimposed, either juxtaposed with, or substituting, the old one, creating all departments and posts necessary for a healthy administration. A lucid legislation, an orderly public revenue, a balanced budget, chief clerks to put affairs straight, civil controllers to check the caïds, and police to keep order, made up the strength of the reformed State. A French, Italian and Maltese population settled in the country and the economic development was spectacular. Railways, roads, ports and later aerodromes facilitated the circulation of wealth throughout the country and exchange with the rest of the world. Power stations were built, to which in recent years great dams have been added, enabling the towns to be electrified. Supplies of water and gas fulfilled urban needs. The piastre, the old Tunisian currency, was replaced by the franc, and the ' Banque de l'Algérie ' was conceded the privilege of issue. Public, semi-public and private credit systems multiplied, and French capital was invested in all sectors of activity. The subsoil, when prospected, revealed resources of phosphate, iron, lead and zinc. On the land settled either by private initiative or State aid, modern forms of improvement appeared: as the acreage sowed with wheat and barley, vineyards, and citrus fruit and olive tree plantations increased, so did the yield. The first modernized industries, with machines run by steam, oil and electricity, began to handle agricultural or mining products; flour mills, vegetable oil refineries, canning factories, cement works, lead foundries, fertilizer factories. Thus the volume of exterior commerce was enlarged on the basis of greater production. Public health also made distinct progress: thanks to more hospitals and a team of doctors, it became easy to foresee or to arrest the great epidemics of plague, cholera or typhus which before had killed large numbers of the population. (Under the impetus of Nicolle, the Pasteur Institute in Tunis became a remarkable research center.) Finally, the country was given a modern public educational system, from primary to secondary, professional and advanced, and recently it was opened to the science and culture of our times.

However, in spite of the positive things that colonization brought — one measures them better today — it was inevitable that it should be criticized. These unequivocal improvements primarily served the colonizers, who predominated in banks, public services, mines, industry and even agriculture — due to their seizure of the most fertile land from which the original owners had often been evicted. The orientation of private investment, the credit policy, the customs system, made Tunisian economy complementary to that of France; and the influx of merchandise from the mother country brought with it an irremediable decadence in skilled workmanship. Industrial development which was doubtless not aided by natural conditions remained insufficiently exploited. And the country's exterior commerce conserved its colonial structure, exporting agricultural or mining products, importing manufactured goods. Also, next to a modern sector where capital and machines assured large profits, there was a traditional sector which, due to routine and lack of credit, continued with unprofitable, archaic techniques. The Administration took, late in the day, measures to make the land productive, to furnish hydraulic equipment, to organize cooperatives, to give financial aid, and these would have helped relieve the conditions of the peasants, but the effort was inadequate. Had it been greater there still would have been the difficulty of overcoming the inertia and distrust of the crude and miserable rural population.

The network of schools was insufficient; alongside a modern French education, the medieval Arab teachings of the Koranic schools and the Great Mosque of Tunis authorized an education for only a small portion of Tunisian children of school age (one boy in three, and one girl in nine, in 1955); in the country especially, illiteracy prevailed. Now, in spite of gaps in hospital organization, the introduction of modern medicine has lowered the mortality rate without modifying the families' attitude towards a respect for life; the balance, periodically re-established before by internal wars, famines and epidemics, is upset. An impulsive birthrate has in a few decades doubled the population. The land still in the possession of Tunisians was reduced to dust by successive divisions; a dry year reduced or destroyed an already poor yield, and hastened the proletarianism of the peasantry: the country was drained of men who could no longer find anything to do. Alongside a working class, whose rights and salaries were guaranteed by law, multiplied a sub-proletariat of laborers in a hopeless search for jobs, who increased the shanty towns on the borders of the big cities; yet whatever the misery of these shacks, they seemed enviable to those who had known the distress of the country. This explosive situation, common to all underdeveloped countries, called for a new economic orientation, a development of agricultural and industrial production, a re-distribution of the sources of wealth, but also an increased effort in education and the reform of institutions and customs of the past, in fact, a mobilization of the masses! A vast program which a colonial state could never carry out, as this would combat interests which it was engaged to serve. And even had it done so, its legitimacy would have been disputed. How could one permit indefinitely a system that had deprived the Tunisian State of all sovereignty, internal and external; which had replaced an absolute monarchy by an omnipotent administration; and had billeted Tunisian officials in the lowest ranks of the hierarchy and excluded them from posts of control; which, in an essentially budgetary Assembly without power of decision — the 'Grand Conseil', created in 1922 and reformed in 1945 — had granted equal representation to a French minority (by direct universal franchise) and to the Tunisian population (by limited, indirect suffrage); which had not even entrusted the administration of the communes to the elected municipalities — and this, when the Tunisian élite was becoming more numerous year by year?

It was in opposition to colonization that the nation gradually united. The nation? Yes, the nation: colonization itself launched it. It had varied the functions of many regions, and linked them by means of fast communication, thus making them interdependent, giving them a unity that they had never had before. The strength and prestige of the colonial state had put an end to the tribes' quarrelsome rivalries and the nomads' sporadic raids against the non-migratory population. The universality of modern law, just or unjust, had shown up the futility of the particularisms of town and province. In spite of social changes which had brought about the formation of a middle class and a proletariat, an entire people had become conscious of having characteristics in common: their past history, the spoken language, the traditions that they respected; through opposition they established themselves. Now, within the regime, young Tunisians manage to do all their classes in the country's schools, and acquire an excellent education in French universities. They could almost forget what binds them to their people and blend instead with a nation whose civilisation fascinates them. But, they will set their faces against this tempting assimilation, so as to do something for their humiliated people, to give a shape to their confused aspirations and to speak in their name. The established powers may treat them as agitators, and those of their companions who preferred to adapt to the new times to grow rich or to seek honors may blame their folly; but today we know that, by their action, the nation has come to life.

One is always interested in origins, and perhaps someone will ask when Tunisian nationalism was born. The beginnings are obscure, but one can give the exact date of the first demonstration at the beginning of this century. The Tekia in Tunis, a home for needy old people was opened on March 24th, 1906. In the presence of the Resident General, Béchir Sfar, president of the *habous*, made the speech. Then after having outlined the spirit and the administration of the home, he dared to say: "The Moslem population fully appreciates the improvements and useful reforms accomplished by the Protectorate Government. We are also equally aware of the measures that the Government is taking to develop charity works and public aid. But we would be much more grateful if, while relieving the misery, our Government would seriously study the means of preventing it. Professional, commercial and agricultural education widely given to the natives; efficient organization and protection of Tunisian labour; protection of local industries by customs measures; finally, the preservation of native property, here, Mr. Governor General, in our humble opinion, are many sure ways of our own to lessen, if not to abolish, the economic crisis which is now raging in the Moslem community." The French representative gave a firm and courteous reply to the speaker. But the colonial press broke out a few days later with the following opinions in *Le Temps:* "Béchir Sfar's words have caused a sensation, because they have put in clear terms the wishes of our dependents and thus officially posed the native question. One of the town's big newspapers has taken offense, and in an extremely sour tone, has contested the right of the natives to complain. Although this always comes from the same group of colonials, but with less and less effect in the colony since the majority joined the democratic party, these attacks make a painful impression on educated Tunisians. The latter, in general are good, peaceful, middle class people, who have a shrewd and positive judgment of affairs, who are thoughtful, who send their sons to our schools, where the young men learn French, assimilate many of our ideas and read our newspapers as we read them ourselves, that is to say, to keep up to date with world news. How distressed and upset they must feel, when, on hearing, in our midst and in our literature, nothing spoken of but justice, liberty, and equality, to see themselves treated as the conquered in such a peremptory fashion. They who have the duty of complete submission and who are given no rights, not even the right to desire, the right to aspire to better circumstances!"

But the " right to desire " took hold. Under the guidance of an enlightened middle class, the national movement grew and grew to gain finally an irrepressible strength. It is enough here to recall — the creation of the evolutionary party in February, 1907, and its dissolution in November, 1911, after the bloody incidents at Djellaz; the foundation of the liberal constitutional party in February, 1920, and the action it took for a constitution 'destour'; the support given by Naceur bey, and the desertion of the sovereign, under pressure from the French authorities, in April, 1921; the long crisis throughout the *destour* after the reforms of July, 1922 — which instituted the " Grand Conseil " — and the dissension which split the old and new teams; the short-lived unity attained by the congress in May, 1933, and the cleavage which, in May, 1934, gave birth at the side of the old *destour* to a *neo-destour*; the orientation, which its leader, Habib Bourguiba, gave to it, and the struggle which developed under the government of the Popular Front; the bloody incidents of April, 1938, and the outlawing of the *neo-destour*; the hopes of the nation just after the war and the inadequacy of the reforms introduced into the country's organization; the increasing authority of the *neo-destour*, which managed once again to carry along the bey in its wake, and the firm but flexible policy that it adopted under the impetus of its leader; the announcement made by France in August, 1950, to grant Tunisia internal self-government, and then her hesitation to keep her promise; the national struggle which started in January, 1952, and the impossibility of ending it by repression or half measures; internal self-government conceded in July, 1954, and the signature of the Franco-Tunisian agreements in June, 1955; finally, the evolution of the North African situation and the solemn recognition of Tunisian independence, March 20, 1956 — nearly fifty years, day for day, after the scandal of the Tekia. The Tunisian poet, Abou-l-Qâsim Chabbi, who died in 1934, at twenty-five and whose verse has just been translated into French, wrote, in one of his most beautiful poems:

Que n'ai-je, ô mon peuple, la force des tempêtes!
Je te jetterais alors la révolte de mon âme.
Que n'ai-je la force des cyclones lorsqu'ils rugissent!
Par mon souffle, je saurais t'inviter à la vie.
Que n'ai-je la force des cyclones!
Mais tu es un être vivant qui passe sa vie dans une tombe.
Tu es une âme stupide qui déteste la lumière
Et traverse les siècles dans une nuit épaisse.
Tu ne peux comprendre si tu ne les touches, si tu ne les palpes,
Les vérités qui marchent autour de toi.

If only I had, oh, my people, the strength of tempests,
I would throw you my soul's rebellion.
If only I had the strength of cyclones when they roar!
With my breath, I would know how to invite you to live.
If only I had the strength of cyclones!
But you are a living being who spends his life in a tomb.
But you are a foolish soul who hates the light
And traverses the centuries in darkest night.
You cannot understand if you do not touch, if you do not feel,
The truths that march around you.

Truth marches, and also arrives. There are those who like to see in Tunisian independence the penalty for colonization's errors. As a matter of fact, it was the necessary end of a movement set in motion in an inert community by the shock of Europe.

5. Dignity regained

On March 25, 1956, a constituent Assembly was elected by direct universal franchise and quickly went to work to decide above all what institutions to give to the country. But without waiting for the working out of a constitution, a new government of which Habib Bourguiba was given the presidency, straightway began to exploit all the conclusions of Tunisia's independence which France had explicitly recognized. Two new departments were created to look after a domain that, in the framework of internal self-government had been exclusively that of France: the Foreign Office, the Ministry of Defense; Tunisia took up direct diplomatic relations with other states and formed an army. Little by little, by means of negotiation with France, everything that was incompatible with the country's new legal status, in the regime defined by the June, 1955, conventions, was revised. The Tunisian government took over all security and police powers, creating a national guard in place of the French Gendarmerie and assumed all the responsibility of supervision of territory and frontier control. An overhaul of regional administration replaced the old caïdates re-grouped under civil supervision, by a new network of governorships, subdivided into delegations giving the governors powers similar to those of the prefects. The old municipalities, appointed under the Protectorate, were replaced by municipal councils elected by direct universal franchise. Everything in the legal organization that could still remind one of the old capitulations in the 'Echelles du Levant' disappeared: Tunisian courts were called in on all civil or penal affairs, whatever the nationality of the parties. The Tunisification of the public offices was briskly expedited; nationals replaced non-nationals in administrative and public services, only technicians and teachers, which the country lacked, remained in office or were freshly recruited from France or other countries. This big change in the institutions had not yet questioned the principle of the monarchy: Lamine bey continued to be, as in the past, the Head of State, investing the President of the Council with his trust and promulgating the legislative papers by the apposition of his seal. But on July 25, 1957, the constituent Assembly, taking into consideration the Husseinite dynasty's past with its dearth of brilliance and grandeur, and the hesitant attitude of the last sovereign during the national struggle, decided to end the beylical regime and solemnly proclaim the republic. The efforts undertaken from 1958 on, to evacuate the French army gradually, did not hinder the construction of a new State which was to receive its basic charter with the constitution, promulgated June 1, 1959, and to come into being with the presidential and legislative elections on November 8th, 1959.

The constitution of the Tunisian Republic asserts the principle of popular sovereignty and its powers are legitimized by universal franchise. Legislative power is exercised by a National Assembly, elected for five years by all citizens of both sexes over the age of twenty-five. Executive power is exercised by a President of the Republic, elected for five years by the same electorate. Through his appointment, the head of State has great prestige and many prerogatives are accorded him. Although he swears to respect the constitution and take care of the nation's interests, he has complete freedom to choose his secretaries of State who are responsible to him, but not to the National Assembly. He sets the general policy of the Government and controls its application. Along with the deputies, he has power to initiate laws; his proposals are given priority for discussion and a two thirds majority is needed to veto them. He promulgates legislative texts, publishes them and sees that they are executed. He appoints civil and military posts; he accredits Tunisian diplomats to foreign powers and foreign diplomats are accredited to him; he ratifies treaties approved by the National Assembly; and in agreement with the latter, he can declare war or make peace, and finally, he is supreme commander of the armed forces. At a time when, in many countries, a traditional parliamentary regime is beginning to show its weaknesses, Tunisian constituents have opted for a presidential regime, giving the country a stable and efficient government. But they show their attachment to democratic principles by affirming the independence of judiciary power, proclaiming the citizens' equality as to their rights and duties and guaranteeing the freedom of fundamental liberties: opinion, press, meetings, and societies. The motto of the Republic is: "Liberty, Order, Justice ".

One hesitates sometimes over the article which makes Islam " the religion of the Republic ", and over the article which states that the head of State should be a Moslem. But in these exceptions to total secularization one should recognize theoretical homage to Islam, a desire to belong to the Moslem community with which, for spiritual and political reasons, they would not wish to break, and not the traces of a theocratic idea or a show of religious intolerance. In fact, the constitution guarantees the freedom of conscience and free exercise of religions. Jews, since time immemorial, have been part of the Tunisian nation, and also Christians. Since new laws have allowed them to ask for and obtain naturalization, they have the same rights and duties as Moslems, under the same civil courts of justice (the religious courts, kept on under the protectorate, have been abolished); there is nothing in their status to remind one of the old statute of the *dhimmis*. Moreover, the organization of the Tunisian republic refers little to Moslem public law. If young Tunisia willingly turns back to the past, it is not to find a model, but to learn a lesson. There is no doubt that structural failings in the in the Islamic States are among the reasons for their decadence at the beginning of modern times. Would a simple return to the teachings of the Prophet have been sufficient for them to recover their greatness? Habib Bourguiba, who has great influence over his people, thinks not. One cannot draw a stable governmental principle from the Koran. But even if one could, it would be dangerous today to adopt the standards of thirteen centuries ago. It is better, on the contrary, to liberate the mind from all the shackles that have bound it under cover of dogma, and carefully to study the experience of other peoples so as to find the best solutions to contemporary problems. These principles, which, today are widespread throughout the Islamic world, inspired the Tunisian constitution, a basic charter for a modern state.

It is difficult for a state to reach immediately a perfect balance between liberty and force. One might think that the Tunisian constitution allows too much power to the President of the Republic and too little to the National Assembly; one may also regret the absence of any counterbalance to the destourian party's influence on the political life of the country and the tutelage it exercises over the laborers', farmers', skilled workmen and tradesmen's unions, and the women's and students' associations; one hopes for a freer exchange of opinions and a wider development of constructive criticism. But, one must realize that the country's rebirth called for a strong power to put an end to destructive traditions and apply revolutionary measures even if it meant abolishing privileges and braving unpopularity; that the *neo-destour* wants to be the party of the entire people and intends to replace class selfishness with a policy of national public welfare and that in a country where democracy has no tradition, it was to be feared that criticism might degenerate into open opposition and that the division of the nation would end in chaos. Be that as it may, the Tunisian constitution was presented as a human work open to improvement and the text provides for its own review. Moreover, beyond possible differences, one fact asserts itself: for the first time in history, this people is aware of being master of its own destiny.

There was a time when Tunisians called themselves — and felt themselves — foreigners in their own country. In a few years, we have seen them quicken to a new life. That the red flag adorned with a star and a crescent floats alone over the monuments; that the signposts on the roads, the illuminated signs in the towns, the official correspondence between the citizens and the administration, should be in Arabic; that Tunisians go to vote to elect their president, their deputies or their municipal councillors; that in the press, on the radio, and in newsreels, their élite should have first place; that public holidays celebrated enthusiastically throughout the year commemorate events in their history; that the State should be represented in international organizations and should make its voice heard in the United Nations; that it is enough for the young to be gifted, to work, to pass their exams, to win competitions, in order to lay claim to responsibility and the highest offices; this is what independence means, this *istiqlâl* chanted formerly by ardent crowds at meetings and public demonstrations.

I no longer know which observer it was who noted that, in the newly liberated countries of Southeast Asia, where English is spoken, the word the heads of State use the most frequently 'is dignified'. The Arab term *karâma,* which means dignity, often comes to the lips of the Tunisian President. In one of his speeches, he did not hesitate to say : " Before we were masters of our destiny, the very idea of happiness was unknown to us. " He added, " There is no happiness except in dignity. " The Tunisian people are happy and proud of having regained their dignity.

6. The new era

The youthful State took over the country before setting up all the public institutions. In spite of the difficulties brought about by the Algerian war, which has often strained relations between Tunisia and France and compromised cooperation between the two countries, the nation has much to show to its credit since its independence.

The new administration has established vigilant control of the economic structure and has adapted and developed resources for the real benefit of the country. The road network system has spread over the country: (1955, 9,160 miles; 1959, 9,670 miles.) The railway, state controlled since 1956, has managed to abolish the deficit by replacing steam engines with diesel and diesel electric engines. Modernization of the ports of Tunis-Goulette, Bizerte, Susa and Sfax is continuing, and work is progressing in the secondary ports of Monastir and Mahedia. A big new port has been built at La Skhira, where large ships are already loading Sahara oil from the Edjele pipeline. The Tunis-El Aouina airport is being modernized and extended and other airports and landing strips are being built in many parts of the country. Transportation and electrical facilities have been increased (1955, 2,950 miles; 1959, 3,500 miles); and this should be sufficient to supply the increased consumption foreseen for the future.

Independent Tunisia intends to keep control over her economy. At the end of 1958, she established a Mint, the Central Bank of Tunisia, and a national currency, the dinar. The State has a large share in such new concerns as the 'Société Tunisienne de Banque', the 'Banque

Nationale Agricole', and the 'Société Nationale d'Investissements', so that distribution of credit corresponds to national interest. The customs union with France has ended, and since August, 1959, there is an autonomous tariff control — save where preferential tariffs have been agreed to by negotiation — which allows free entry for all industrial equipment and at the same time shields the productions of overly young industries from overly severe competition. All these measures were seen as necessary to the country's development.

The restoration of political sovereignty has opened the way to an economic recovery which will certainly continue to grow. The nationalization of the railways has been followed by the nationalization of tramways, trolleys and buses which serve the large towns, of the production and distribution of gas and electricity, and of the road system. The State owns half the shares in the Gafsa Rail and Phosphates Company as well as in its offshoot, the Company of Phosphoric Acid and Fertilizers. As a result of negotiation with the French Government, large pieces of land have been handed over to the Tunisian state, which is allotting them either to 'fellahs' with no land of their own or to cooperative groups of workers under a supervisor. The French have been encouraged by this new climate to sell to Tunisians, — building plots, industrial plants and businesses, — wealth is being transferred, but the national revenue is still so small that no amount of redistribution will increase the standard of living. The revenue of 209,3 million dinars, or 55 dinars per head per annum must be increased by increasing production.

Efforts in this direction are mainly concerned with agricultural production. The state has widely encouraged the acquisition of *habous* land, target of radical reform, estates and collectivities, by those of precarious means or by uprooted 'fellahs' who are given financial and technical aid on condition of improved yields. For the development of the Medjerda valley, begun under the protectorate, an agrarian reform was needed — passed by law, June, 1958. This project will, by irrigating some 125,000 acres, allow the soil to be cultivated in an intensive rather than an extensive fashion. A similar project will be launched in the Oued Nebana valley, where a dam will be built to irrigate 15,000 acres. In a less spectacular way, the boring of artesian wells, the excavating of surface wells and the multiplying of small dams have created little cultivated areas like artificial oases in a land which suffers from an insufficient and irregular rainfall. The whole nation has been mobilized to prevent and repair erosion. The administration distributes, and the farmers use, the means best fitted for the work; contour plowing, stubble conservation, the use of pronged farm implements and the rotation of crops. Forests are better protected against spoliation, notably by the ban on goat grazing. The reforestation of the country is considered of first importance, and everywhere the traveler sees young plantations bringing life to the desolate landscape. A wider distribution of credit; an advance in the teaching and popularization of agriculture; adoption in each region of the most suitable means of cultivation; the development of rational breeding methods; the progress of cooperative farming which brings modern techniques to the small farmer, all this will in the long run bring about a notable increase in agricultural and stock production.

Meanwhile, Tunisia attaches great importance to the prospecting of the subsoil — the search for oil is vigorously pursued — and modernization of the equipment for her deposits of phosphates, iron, lead, zinc and salt. The hope is to enlarge the scope of her conversion industries. The ban on the importation of shoes has encouraged local manufacturers who use leather tanned locally. A factory at Kasserine will transform alfa from the steppes into cellulose for export, another at Béjà will first handle imported raw sugar, and later, the sugar beet crop which will be grown in the Medjerda valley. A factory at La Skhira will refine imported crude oil — until some may be discovered in Tunisia — to supply her needs for gasoline, fuel-oil and other byproducts. A textile combine at Ksar Hellal is already making cotton material with imported thread, and a spinning factory at Susa will shortly supply this thread, and eventually, after an experimental phase, with cotton grown on the spot. Many more examples could be added to this list, but this suffices to show the latent industrial possibilities which are being realized. At the same time there is a re-organization of the handicrafts industry designed to improve the quality of the local arts and crafts — carpets, handwoven materials, embroidery, pottery — and to bring them a bigger market. Traditional fishing has had its equipment and methods brought more into line under the protection of a government office. Tourism and its facilities are improving, thanks to intelligent propaganda and methodical organization which has, among other things, modernized and extended inadequate hotel accommodation.

Although these many marks of progress have already reduced the chronic deficit of the trade balance, an increase in production is not sufficient in itself to raise personal income. It must increase faster than the rise in population, — 2% per year. This obligation, common to all underdeveloped countries, is clearly understood by responsible Tunisians, and the time seems to have come to decide on a coherent plan of development for which the basic data, the coordination of fundamental studies and pilot schemes already exist. But where can the capital be found for the necessary investment? France has been obliged to defer the financial aid she had promised. The United States has only partly replaced it, and the valuable aid given by the United Nations has, of political necessity, been mainly technical. Tunisia has hesitated to accept the offer of loans in material and goods from the Eastern countries, although she has diplomatic and trade relations with them. While waiting for greater aid from the outside world, the country is making big efforts to help herself. The spread of modern loan facilities, much encouraged, can increase the available means of credit houses. Healthy management of public finance can give greater spending power to the state. Here and now, tens of thousands of unemployed have been given regular work on special projects, for a modest salary, part cash, part in kind, and have been saved from lives of idleness and hunger. If this huge potential, within the framework of the development scheme, is used to the greatest possible advantage, it will show a profitable return. Investing in labor may be a shortcut to the rapid build-up of national capital in underdeveloped countries. "Capital is made at home," said the economist Nurske.

Important progress has been made with social problems. The hospital network reorganization has resulted in an increase in the number of beds; 1955, 6,355; 1959, 10,539. There are more dispensaries to carry on the fight against illness and to see that proper care is given; 1955, 101; 1959, 405. Money has been given, and new methods employed, in the fight against tuberculosis and trachoma. The founding of centers for the care of mothers and infants has increased pre-natal consultations and spread principles of child welfare. Children abandoned by their parents, once potential delinquents, are now grouped in reception centers and special villages, where, fed and clothed, they are given primary education and taught a trade. Begging has disappeared, partly because of security measures, but also thanks to the increased assistance given to the old and infirm and to the jobs provided for the unemployed by the state. School canteens and the methodical distribution of milk and bread rations are saving the most vulnerable members of the community from malnutrition. Simultaneously the state, the governorships, the communes are improving housing conditions; in the country solid *meljas* are replacing shacks, and in the towns unsanitary blocks and shanties are razed and the workers rehoused in healthy new housing projects. Finally, a start is being made in town planning, and most strikingly in the capital itself. The making of new streets, demolition of ancient city walls, broadening of streets and transforming of disused cemeteries into gardens and squares is all going forward towards the equipment and adaptation of the towns to a modern way of life. It is true that the government's objective to press forward with economic expansion has led it to check the drive for trade unionism, but Tunisian workers have been granted an agricultural statute, a recasting of the laws governing accident and sickness benefits, as well as social security. Moreover, the drop in total unemployment, thanks to government planning and the projects already mentioned, must be counted on the credit side if one wants to appreciate intelligently the evolution of the Tunisian worker.

State schools have been reorganized, by a statute of education which coordinates the curriculae at the primary, intermediate and secondary level. Teaching has a national bias; Arabic being the common language, more time is given to the study of Arab culture and facts of the Maghreb. A modern outlook is expressed in the teaching as well as in the subjects taught. There are no more Koran schools, and the Great Mosque of Tunis has stopped giving its medieval instruction to thousands of young people. Nevertheless, French is taught even in the primary schools as it is realized that an early understanding of that language, which is for the moment used in intermediate and secondary schools, is necessary now and for some time to those who pursue higher education. Thanks to the budget allocation, the government, aided by the local councils and population, has been able to build and open new schools. The number of those who have a primary education grows each year, (a 50% increase between 1955 and 1959). At the moment two out of four boys and three out of four girls are being educated and it seems reasonable to suppose that in ten years every child will have been taught to read. Intermediate and secondary education also show marked progress. The founding of a University of Tunis, with varied department, and soon with institutes for pure and applied research, in close cooperation with France will offer Tunisia complete higher education. A recent conference of Tunisian intellectuals of all fields was called to discuss results of, as well as the outlook on, scientific research. Meanwhile, for illiterates, there are short courses teaching various trades which help that generation of adults who did not have the same opportunities as the youth of today.

The rights of the family, till now based on the Koran, are being reformed and brought up-to-date in a liberal manner. A new law has suppressed the absolute power a father had over his daughter or a guardian over his ward, made the consent of women a necessary condition to marriage, and permits marriage between people of different religions, which up till now has been impossible. Polygamy is now a punishable offense, legal divorce has replaced the one-sided repudiation by the husband. Adoption is now legal, and women have had their rights of succession and inheritance restored and increased. All these innovations which give greater equality of the sexes and more individual freedom in a traditionally patriarchal society are considered by all Islam specialists to be the most revolutionary and daring ever to be adopted by any Arab country. At the same time pressure is being brought to bear to abolish the veil, — never prescribed by Islam, but which dogged tradition has enforced. The head of state has, with all his authority, unhesitatingly condemned this " miserable rag ". Woman's emancipation, such as her political freedom, which is established by her new legal status, is resisted by the women themselves. Did one not see during the last century liberated slaves wishing to return to slavery? The young generation of women, who have been educated, walk bare-headed and coat less, earn their living, and accept this freedom with open arms. Although it may take time for the new ways to be assimilated, the Tunisian family is here and now irrecoverably committed to this evolution.

This questioning of ancestral ways and customs is not limited to family life; it includes dress, housing and manners. (The lengthy, flowery greeting is forbidden in public offices.) Tradition which only yesterday seemed a haven from too harsh reality is now seen as a humiliating reminder of the past. New values are taking the place of old. The serenity of faith has yielded to the restlessness of research, resignation, to creative effort; the taste for techniques replaces meditations on eternity; and, as a curious paradox, although Arabic is now the official language, more French is being learned, as the educated young discover that it opens the doors to the knowledge and experience of more advanced peoples. Of course, these changes affect only a small élite section of the people, but this élite, which is growing every day, will certainly form the nation in its own image. In spite of her affinity for the Arab and Islamic States, young Tunisia wishes to become Westernized, that is to say, to assume the universal ideals the West can offer. Long ago, an Indian, Mohammed Iqbal, remarked that the Islamic world was moving spiritually westward, but today the only measure is the speed with which political liberation brings Westernization.

Habib Bourguiba, speaking in the Great Kairouan Mosque at the religious ceremony of Mouled, praised the human motive that had made it possible for the first rocket to reach the moon, and affirmed the right "to liberate Islamic principles from their framework of outmoded demands." Shortly after, he persuaded Tunisians to continue to work during the month of Ramadan. If fasting hindered their work, they should make use of the derogations provided for by their religion. When the Prophet marched on Mecca, did he not tell his warriors to break their fast, and did not he, himself, preach the example, so that they should not meet the enemy in a weakened state? But, if one is allowed not to fast during *jihâd*, a holy war, should one not assimilate to *jihâd* the fight for economic development and social recovery? This interpretation is striking in its audacity. In the Middle Ages, Moslem philosophy had already distinguished the little *jihâd*, or struggle against an adversary, from the great *jihâd*, or struggle against oneself. But this time, the great *jihâd* is no longer an individual effort to attain virtue, it is the whole nation's efforts "to catch up with the procession of civilized nations".

Without doubt, the life of the European minority was disturbed by independence and national reconstruction, and many of them left the country. But the Tunisian Government has avoided brutal measures and the French made the necessary changes easier. With revolutions — and decolonization is one — not everything is perfect. And legitimacy does not come first and foremost when a revolution opens the gates of a new age for a people.

One must ask some questions about the future of Tunisia. The 1959 constitution shows it as "part of united Maghreb". Is it called upon to unite with Algeria and Morocco? The three countries border on each other, and as the frontiers are only political, they form one territory. With only slight differences the same sort of natural conditions and same way of life exist. From the Mediterranean to the Atlantic, the basic population is Berber, Arabized and Islamized, colonized by the same power. Even if they speak different Arab dialects, with some important Berber language centers — in Algeria and Morocco — classic Arabic, or even French, permit an exchange from east to west. The unity of the three countries would, without doubt, help their economic and social construction, and it would increase their weight in the modern world. However, one generally bases on a common history the objective foundation of any real nation. Although analogies exist between the countries and the peoples of North Africa, one must realize that they have had, until now, separate histories, from which each country and each people draws its individuality. If therefore, Maghreb is eventually united, we see it rather as a federation of states and not as a single state. Although political notions and the will of man may mock at historical evidence, we remain conscious of that which each nation possesses innately. We believe we recognize in the Tunisian personality the working of a unique destiny, from Carthage to to-morrow.

Paul Sebag

Some Figures

- *Area :*
  Tunisia, 164,150 km².
  (Algeria : 2,195,098 km² and Morocco: 520,380 km².)

- *Productive area :*
  The productive surface totals approx. 9,000,000 ha, as ff.: arable land: 4,000,000 ha (44.4%); natural prairies: 105,000 ha, (1.2%); tree and shrub cultivation, 912,000 ha (10.1%); woods and forest: 980,000 ha (10.9%); grazing land and cultivated, nonproductive land: 3,003,000 ha (33.4%).

- *Population :*
  The census of Feb. 1, 1956, establishes the population at 3,783,169 inhabitants; by nationality — Moslem Tunisians: 3,383,904; Jewish Tunisians: 57,792; non-Tunisian Moslems: 86,149; French: 180,440; Italians: 66,910; other Europeans: 7,974. By the end of 1958 there were only 146,000 Europeans, — 86,000 French; 53,000 Italians and 7,000 other.

- *Demographic structure :*
  Tunisian pop. divided into age groups: 0 to 19 years.: 52%; 20 to 39 years.: 29%; 40 to 59 years.: 14%; over 60 years.: 5%.

- *Active population :*
  The active Tunisian pop., totalling 1,221,550, is divided into following groups: primary sector, (agriculture) — 72 %; secondary sector, (industrial) — 8%; third sector, (services) — 20%.

- *Cities :*
  Principal cities are: Tunis; pop. 410,000 (Greater Tunis, pop. 550,000); Sfax, pop. 65,635; Susa, pop. 48,172; Bizerta, pop. 44,681; Menzel Bourguiba, pop. 34,732; Kairouan, pop. 33,968; M'saken, pop. 26,142; Gabes, pop. 24,420; Gafsa, pop. 24,345; Béjà, pop. 22,668; Census: Feb. 1, 1956.

- *Roads :*
  At year's end, 1958, the road network was comprised of 8,469 km of paved roads and 7,096 km of unpaved roads, total, 15,565 km.

- *Railway system :*
  Two large networks: the National Company of Tunisian Railroads' system: 1,525 km and the Gafsa Railroad and Phosphate Company system: 455 km. Total: 1,980 km of railroads.

Population density by governorships - Principal cities.

over 100 per km²
fr. 75 - 100 per km²
fr. 50 - 75 per km²
25 - 50 per km²
from 15 - 25 per km²
less than 15 per km²
cities of population over 20,000
cities of population over 10,000

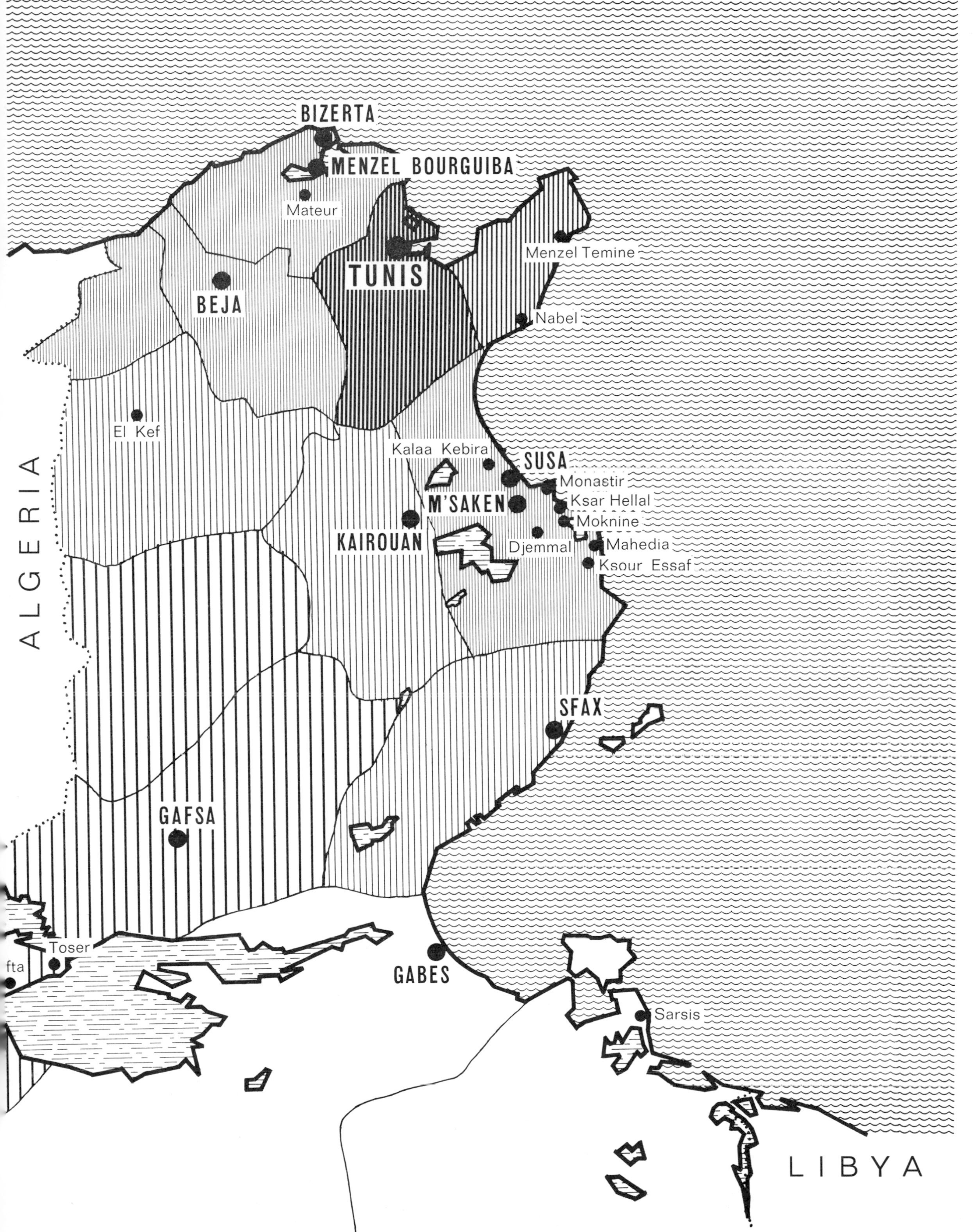

BIZERTA
MENZEL BOURGUIBA
Mateur
Menzel Temine
TUNIS
BEJA
Nabel
El Kef
Kalaa Kebira
SUSA
Monastir
Ksar Hellal
M'SAKEN
Moknine
KAIROUAN
Djemmal
Mahedia
Ksour Essaf
ALGERIA
SFAX
GAFSA
Toser
fta
GABES
Sarsis
LIBYA

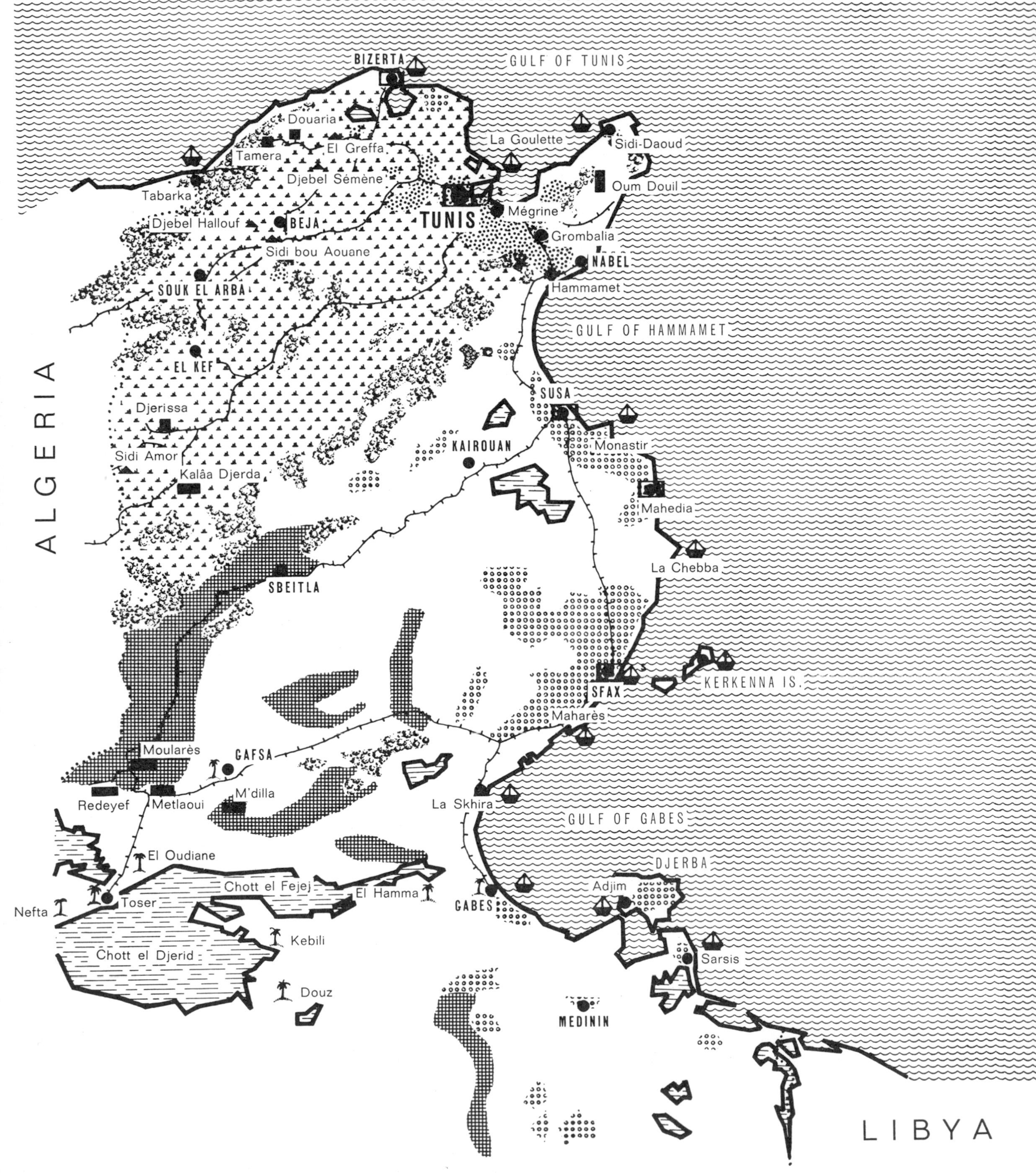

BIZERTA
GULF OF TUNIS
Douaria
El Greffa
Tamera
La Goulette
Sidi-Daoud
Djebel Sémène
Oum Douil
Tabarka
Djebel Hallouf
BEJA
TUNIS
Mégrine
Grombalia
Sidi bou Aouane
NABEL
SOUK EL ARBA
Hammamet
GULF OF HAMMAMET
EL KEF
ALGERIA
SUSA
Djerissa
KAIROUAN
Monastir
Sidi Amor
Kalâa Djerda
Mahedia
La Chebba
SBEITLA
SFAX
KERKENNA IS.
Maharès
Moularès
GAFSA
M'dilla
Redeyef
Metlaoui
La Skhira
GULF OF GABES
El Oudiane
DJERBA
Chott el Fejej
Adjim
El Hamma
GABES
Toser
Nefta
Kebili
Sarsis
Chott el Djerid
Douz
MEDININ
LIBYA

• *Harbors :*

Four principal ports in order of importance — Tunis, (imp. 710,000 T. — exp. 1,817,000 T.) Sfax, (imp. 203,000 T. — exp. 2,018,000 T.); Bizerta, (imp. 23,000 T. — exp. 251,000 T.); Susa, (imp. 25,000 T. — exp. 145,000 T.). Figures for 1958.

• *Energy :*

Production of electrical energy furnished by power stations representing power equipment for 110,000 kw., of which 85,000 kw. for the rural stations and 25,000 kw. for hydraulic stations. Electrical consumption in 1958 totaled 235,000,000 kwh., 60 kwh. per person per year.

• *Agriculture :*

During 1958 Tunisian agriculture consisted of — wheat : 1,109,000 ha (4,143,000 qtls); soft wheat: 174,000 ha (1,243,000 qtls); barley: 804,000 ha (2,817,000 qtls); olives : 19,500,000 trees in production, (1,200,000 qtls olive oil and 165,000 qtls derived oils); vineyards : 42,100 ha (1,950,000 hl of wine); date palms: 3,348,000 trees, (460,000 qtls, dates); citrus fruit: 2,060,000 trees (730,000 qtls oranges, lemons, tangerines); other fruit : 11,020,000 trees (830,000 qtls, fruit); tobacco : 1,709 ha (15,690 qtls).

• *Stock breeding :*

1958 : Livestock in Tunisia incl. 562,700 cattle; 3,410,000 sheep; 1,447,000 goats; plus 313,700 horses, donkeys and mules and 211,600 camels.

• *Fishing industry :*

Production: sardines, allache-sardines, anchovies — 7,363 T., other: 6,897 T.; tuna — 677 T. and sponges — 160 T. (1958).

• *Extraction industries :*

This production includes 2,278,000 T. phosphates; 1,103,000 T. iron ore; 35,000 T. lead ore; 6,074 zinc ore; 170,000 T. sea salt; (1958).

• *Conversion Industries :*

Some production figures, (1958): soft lead: 25,100 T., metal containers: 3,790 T., cement: 345,000 T., lime : 72,000 T., superphosphates : 142,000 T., hyperphosphates : 101,000 T., manufactured tobacco : 2,841 T., soap : 8,800 T., wrapping paper : 4,040 T., beer: 113,000 hl tinned vegetables: 5,087 T., tinned fruit: 5,825 T., tinned fish: 5,060 T.

Natural resources and production

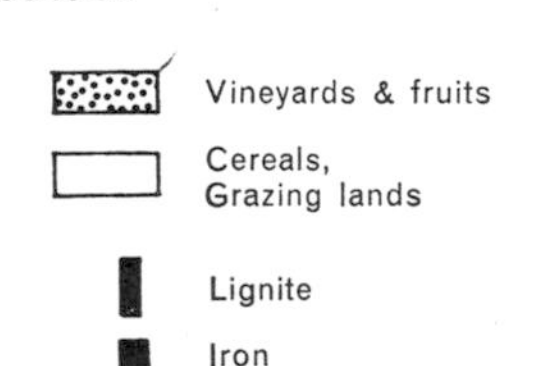

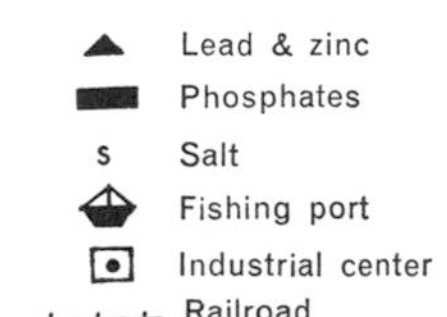

• *Handicraft industries :*

Principal production: rugs (Kairouan, Oudref, El Djem; decorative weaving (El Djem, Djebiniana); blankets, (Gafsa, Djerba); lace and embroidery, (Tunis, Nabel); glazed ceramics, (Nabel); chased copper and brass, (Tunis); jewelry (Tunis).

• *Exchange :*

Exports : cereals, fruits and vegetables, olive oil, wine and liquor, alfa, phosphates and phosphatized fertilizer, soft lead, cement, tinned fruits, vegetables, fish.

Imports : cereals, sugar, coffee, tea, tobacco, wood, coal, gasoline, fuel-oil, steel and other metals, tools and machines, cloth and clothing, medicines and chemical products, paper and cardboard, automobiles.

• *Commercial balance :*

1958 *: Imports :* 64,9 million dinars distrib. — franc zone: 78%; dollar zone: 3%; sterling zone: 5%; other: 14%; *Exports :* 64,4 million dinars, distrib. — franc zone: 69%; dollar zone: 2%; sterling zone: 7%; other: 22%.

• *Currency :*

National currency is the dinar subdivided into 1,000 millimes. In 1960 : 1 dollar equaled 0,416 dinar; 1 pound sterling — 1,164 dinar; 10 French NF — 0,845 d.; 10 DM — 0,990 d.; 10 Swiss frs. equaled. 0,950 d., and 1,000 It. lira — 0,665 dinar.

• *National Income :*

Gross national product of Tunisia was calculated at 209,3 million dinars, as follows: agriculture: 72,1; extraction industries: 9,3; manufacturing industries: 23,8; construction: 9,5; electricity, gas and water: 3,8; transportation and communication: 17,3; commerce and banks: 44,8; other services: 28,7 millions. (Average 1955-58.)

• *Tourist industry :*

During the year 1959 Tunisia received approx. 50,000 tourists of the following nationalities: French: 44,3%; German: 13,3%; Italian: 8,7%; Scandinavian: 5%; American: 4,6%; British: 4,4%; Swiss: 3,6%; other: 16,1%

Relief Alt.

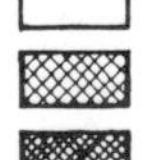

less than 200 m.
more than 200 m.
more than 500 m.

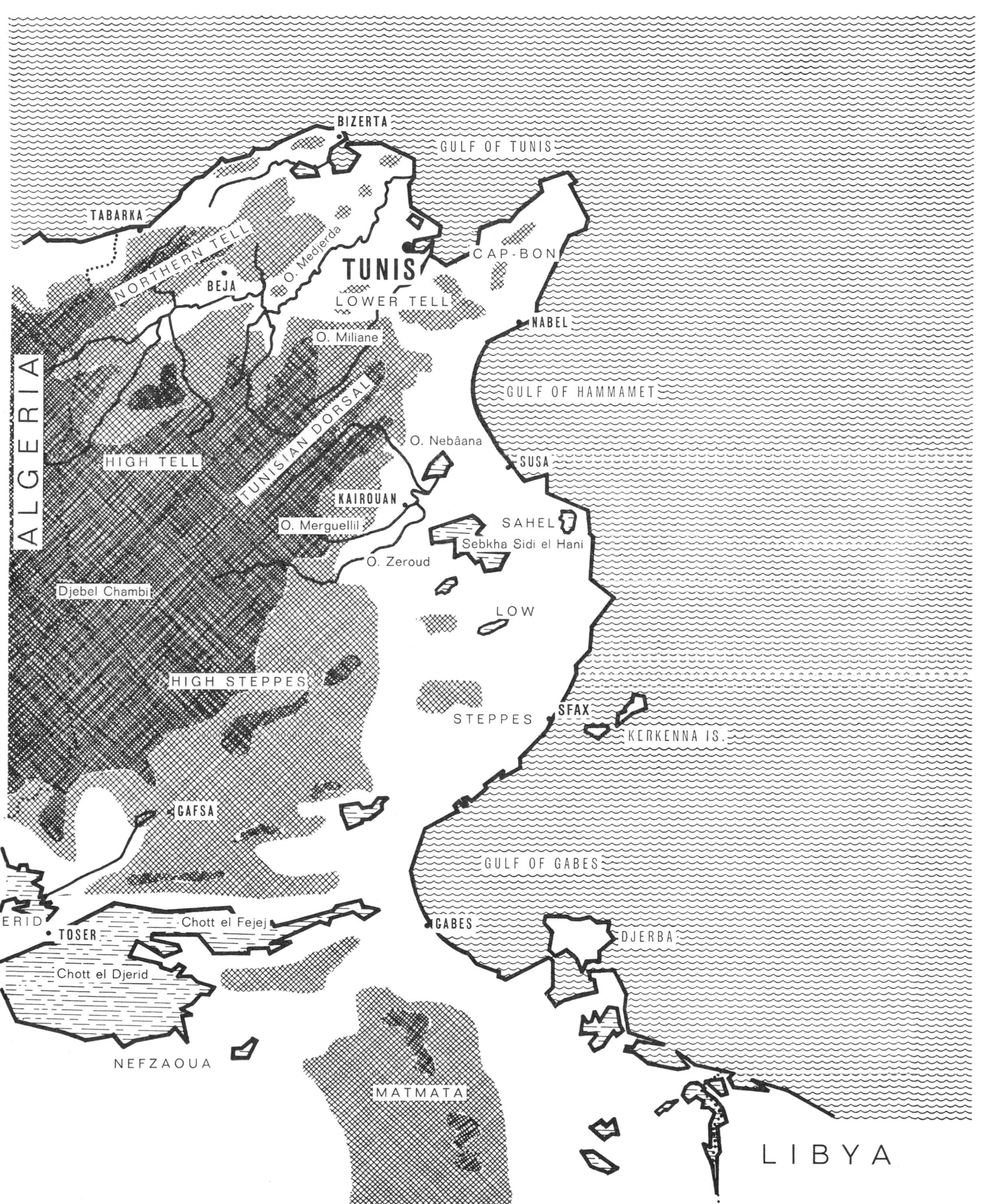
BIZERTA
GULF OF TUNIS
TABARKA
NORTHERN TELL
O. Medjerda
BEJA
TUNIS
CAP-BON
LOWER TELL
NABEL
O. Miliane
ALGERIA
GULF OF HAMMAMET
TUNISIAN DORSAL
O. Nebâana
HIGH TELL
SUSA
KAIROUAN
SAHEL
O. Merguellil
Sebkha Sidi el Hani
O. Zeroud
Djebel Chambi
LOW
HIGH STEPPES
STEPPES
SFAX
KERKENNA IS.
GAFSA
GULF OF GABES
ERID
TOSER
Chott el Fejej
GABES
DJERBA
Chott el Djerid
NEFZAOUA
MATMATA
LIBYA

References

Photographs

INGE MORATH: pp. 19, 20, 21, 24, 25, 28, 29, 32-33, 36, 37, 38, 41, 42, 43, 45, 46-47, 48, 49, 51, 55, 56, 61, 62-63, 66, 68, 69, 70, 71, 73, 75, 76-77, 78, 80, 82, 84, 85, 86-87, 88, 89, 90, 92-93, 94, 95, 97, 98, 99, 100, 104, 105, 106, 107, 110, 111, 112, 113, 114, 116-117, 120, 123, 125, 128.

ANDRÉ MARTIN: pp. 22-23, 30, 35, 52-53, 54, 60, 65, 81, 96, 102-103, 109, 118-119.

MARC RIBOUD: pp. 26-27, 64, 121, 122, 126.

Texts

P. 16: R. P. DAN: *Histoire de Barbarie et de ses corsaires.* P. Rocolet. Paris. 1637. / p. 18: IBN FADHL ALLAH AL-'OMARÎ: *Masâlik el abçâr fî mamâlik el amçâr,* trans. Gaudefroy-Demombynes. Geuthner. Paris. 1927. / pp. 24, 25, 49, 54, 98, 118, 119: J. QUEMENEUR: *Énigmes tunisiennes.* S.A.P.I. Tunis. 1944. / p. 27: B. ROY et P. POINSSOT: *Inscriptions arabes de Kairouan.* Klincksieck. Paris. 1950-1958. / p. 28: A. GIDE: *Les Nourritures terrestres.* Bibliothèque de la Pléiade. Gallimard. Paris. 1958. / p. 31: G. DUHAMEL: *Le Prince Jaffar:* Mercure de France. Paris. 1924. / p. 34: trans. in J. et S. COMBES, A. LOUIS: *Autour du travail de la laine.* Revue de l'Institut des Belles Lettres Arabes. Tunis. 1946. / p. 36: PLAUTE: *Théâtre.* Le Carthaginois. Les Belles Lettres. Paris. / p. 39: trans. in A. DEMEERSEMAN: *Tunisie, sève nouvelle.* Casterman. Paris. 1957. / pp. 40, 57: Adaptation by Cl. Roy, from P. MARTY: *Chants lyriques populaires du Sud tunisien.* Revue Tunisienne, Tunis. 1936-1937. / p. 43: *Le Koran :* trans. M. Kasimirski. Fasquelle. Paris (s. d.) / p. 48: IBN-'ABD-ALHAKAM: *Conquête de l'Afrique du Nord et de l'Espagne,* trans. A. Gateau. Carbonel. Algiers. 2nd ed. 1948. / p. 50: ABOU-L-'ARAB: *Classes des savants de l'Ifrîqiya,* trans. M. Ben Cheneb. Carbonel Algiers. 1920. / p. 58: SEGHIR BEN YOUSSEF: *Mechra el Melki,* trans. V. Serres, M. Lasram. Imprimerie Rapide Tunis. 1900. / p. 61: *Corpus Inscriptionum latinarum,* trans. in CH. A. JULIEN: *Histoire de l'Afrique du Nord.* Payot. Paris. 2nd ed. 1951. / p. 64: TERTULLIEN: *Apologétique :* trans. J.P. Waltzing. Les Belles Lettres. Paris. 1929. / p. 65: A. RENON: *Les Semailles.* Namura. Tunis. 1944. / p. 67: A. HUXLEY: *The Olive Tree and Other Essays,* pub. by Chatto and Windus, London, 1947 / p. 68: PLINY THE ELDER: *Natural History.* / p. 71: APULÉE. *L'Ane d'or,* trans. by P. Yalette. Les Belles Lettres. Paris. 1947. / p. 72: trans. A. Louis. Revue de l'Institut des Belles Lettres Arabes. Tunis. 1944. / p. 74: trans. J. Cuoq. Revue de l'Institut des Belles Lettres Arabes. Tunis. 1944. / p. 79: DIODORE DE SICILE: *Bibliothèque historique,* trans. Hoefer. Delahays. Paris. 1851. / p. 80: *Pirke Aboth. Traité des principes ou Recueil de préceptes et de sentences des pères de la Synagogue,* trans. A. Créhange. Durlacher. Paris. 1953. / p. 83: N. SLOUCHZ: *L'île de Djerba.* Dvir. Tel-Aviv. 1957. / pp. 84, 104: SAINT AUGUSTIN: *Confessions,* trans. P. de Labriolle. Les Belles Lettres. Paris. 1925. / p. 88: *Corpus inscriptionum latinarum,* trans. in G. BOISSIER: *L'Afrique Romaine.* Hachette. Paris. 1901. / pp. 89, 123: APULÉE: *Les Florides,* trans. H. Clouard. Garnier. Paris. (s. d.) / p. 91: VIRGILE: *Les Géorgiques,* trans. P.-A. Nicolas. Les Belles Lettres. Paris. 1948. / p. 94: VIRGIL: *Aeneid.* / p. 96: PROCOPE: *Guerres de Justinien,* trans. M. Fumée. Michel Sonnius. Paris. 1587. / p. 99: HOMÈRE: *L'Odyssée :* trans. V. Bérard. A. Colin. Paris. 1942. / p. 101: A. F. CIRNI: *Della presa delle Gerbe,* trans. in CH. MONCHICOURT: *L'expédition espagnole de 1560 contre l'île de Djerba.* E. Leroux. Paris. 1913. / p. 106: MANILIUS: *Astronautics.* / p. 107: PENTADIUS, trans. in P. MONCEAUX: *Les Africains.* Lecène, Oudin et Cie. Paris. 1894. / p. 108: SANDOVAL: *Historia de la vida y hechos del emperador Carlo V.* Valladolid. 1606. / p. 110: J.-A. PEYSSONNEL: *Relation d'un voyage sur les côtes de Barbarie fait par ordre du roi en 1724 et 1725,* pub. M. Dureau de la Malle. Faivre. Paris. 1838. / p. 111: PLINY THE YOUNGER: *Letters.* / p. 112: JUSTIN: *Histoire universelle,* trans. Abbé Paul. Chambeau. Avignon. 1810. / p. 115: M.-L. DUBOULOZ-LAFFIN: *Le Bou Mergoud. Folklore tunisien.* G.-P. Maisonneuve. Paris. 1946. / p. 120: EN NOWEIRÎ: *Nihayat al-arab,* trans. M. de Slane in IBN KHALDOUN: *Histoire des Berbères et des dynasties musulmanes de l'Afrique septentrionale.* Geuthner. Paris. 1925. / p. 122: EL ABDERI: *Rihla,* trans. M. Cherbonneau. Revue Tunisienne, Tunis. 1905. / p. 124: H. BOURGUIBA: *Le destour et la France.* Épinay-sur-Seine. 1937. / p. 126: ABOU-L-QÂSIM CHABBI trans. A. Ghedira. P. Seghers. Paris. 1959. / p. 129: G. DE MAUPASSANT: *La Vie errante.* Albin Michel. Paris.

This book was produced by Robert Delpire and Jacques Monory.
Printed March 10, 1962 by Draeger Frères, Paris.
And bound by Engel, Malakoff.